Holt French

Grammar Tutor
for Students of French

Levels 1, 2, and 3

HOLT, RINEHART AND WINSTON
A Harcourt Education Company

Austin • Orlando • Chicago • New York • Toronto • London • San Diego

Contributing Writer

Dr. Cherie Mitschke
Southwestern University

Cover Photography Credits
(t) © Dana White/PhotoEdit/Picture Quest; (b) Digital Imagery® © 2003 PhotoDisc, Inc.

ALLEZ, VIENS! is a trademark licensed to Holt, Rinehart and Winston, registered in the United States of America and/or other jurisdictions.

Printed in the United States of America

ISBN 0-03-065668-0

1 2 3 4 5 6 7   066   05 04 03 02 01

Table of Contents

French 1

Table of Contents *continued*

French 2

Table of Contents continued

French 3

To the Teacher

Many students do not have a clear understanding of their own language and cannot, therefore, build on that understanding as they learn a second language. The intention of this *Grammar Tutor* is to explain the basic grammar concepts introduced and practiced in *Allez, viens!* first in English, with English examples and activities, and then in French, so that students can relate the concept to something they do every day in English and thereby gain insights about how the grammar works before they attempt to learn it in the context of an entirely new language.

The *Grammar Tutor* presents in sequential order the main grammar points introduced in *Allez, viens!*, Levels 1, 2, and 3. These grammar points are compared to English as appropriate, so that students can readily see the many similarities between the two languages. In some cases, they will, of course, see differences; however, as they compare and contrast the structures of French and English, they will no doubt accomplish one goal: they will increase their understanding of language in general and become better able to use it to communicate.

The explanation of each grammar concept is accompanied by examples, and each presentation is followed by an activity that allows students to verify that they have understood the explanation of the grammar concept. The concepts are presented first in English and then in French; the activity following the presentation has the same format in both languages, to enable students to quickly see the comparison between the two languages.

Following the initial activity is an activity that asks students to apply what they understood from the presentation. The final activity on each Activity Master encourages students to think about both the target language and their own.

It is the intention of this book to give students more insight into their own language and to help them better understand how their knowledge of English grammar can be transferred to French.

On the following pages is a glossary of the grammar terms that are covered in this book. This "Grammar at a Glance" can serve as a quick reference to the more detailed material covered in the body of the *Grammar Tutor*.

Grammar at a Glance

adjective An adjective modifies a noun or a pronoun. (See also **demonstrative adjective, interrogative adjective,** and **possessive adjective.**)

> EXAMPLES   The Duponts have a **beautiful, red** car.
> *Les Dupont ont une **jolie** voiture **rouge.***

adjective agreement (See **agreement.**)

adverb An adverb modifies a verb, an adjective, or another adverb.

> EXAMPLES   When it's **very** cold, I **often** take the subway.
> *Quand il fait **très** froid, je prends **souvent** le métro.*

agreement Agreement is the correspondence, or match, between grammatical forms. Grammatical forms agree when they have the same number or gender.

subject-verb agreement Subject-verb agreement refers to the form of a verb that goes with its subject.

> EXAMPLES   **This package is** a gift for my mother.
> *Ce **paquet est** un cadeau pour ma mère.*

adjective agreement Adjective agreement refers to the form of an adjective that matches the number and gender of the noun it modifies. English has no adjective agreement, but French adjectives must match the nouns they modify.

> FXAMPLES   **My sister** is **short. My brother** is **short,** too.
> *Ma **sœur** est **petite. Mon frère** est **petit** aussi.*

article An article refers to a noun. Articles are the most frequently used type of adjectives.

definite article A definite article refers to a specific noun.

> EXAMPLES   **The** kitten won't come down from **the** tree.
> *Le petit chat ne veut pas descendre de **l'**arbre.*

indefinite article An indefinite article refers to a noun that is not specific.

> EXAMPLES   They ordered **a** pie and **a** cake.
> *Ils ont pris **une** tarte et **un** gâteau.*

partitive article A partitive article refers to some or part of something. English uses "some" to express the partitive.

> EXAMPLES   Martha bought **some** bread, **some** jam, and **some** mineral water.
> *Marthe a acheté **du** pain, **de la** confiture et **de l'**eau minérale.*

command (See **imperative mood.**)

conditional The conditional verb form is used to tell what you would or would not do under certain conditions.

> EXAMPLES   If I had the money, I **would buy** this book.
> *Si j'avais de l'argent, j'**achèterais** ce livre.*

contraction A contraction is a shortened form of a word, numeral, or a group of words. Apostrophes in contractions indicate where letters or numerals have been omitted.

    EXAMPLES   **I'm** thirteen years old.

                      J'ai treize ans.

definite article (See **article.**)

demonstrative adjective A demonstrative adjective points out a specific person, place, thing, or idea.

    EXAMPLES   Do you prefer **this** coat or **that** vest?

                      *Tu préfères **ce** manteau ou **cette** veste?*

demonstrative pronoun A demonstrative pronoun stands for a specific person, place, thing, or idea.

    EXAMPLES   I like **these.**

                      *J'aime **ceux-là.***

direct object A direct object is a word or word group that receives the action of the verb or shows the result of the action. A direct object answers the question *Whom?* or *What?* after a verb of action.

    EXAMPLES   My parents rarely watch **television.**

                      *Mes parents regardent rarement **la télévision.***

direct object pronoun (See **pronoun.**)

imperative mood A sentence in the imperative gives a command or makes a request.

    EXAMPLES   **Do** your homework! **And then, let's go** to the movies.

                      ***Fais** tes devoirs! **Ensuite, allons** au cinéma.*

imperfect The imperfect tense refers to actions or conditions in the past that were ongoing, that occurred regularly, or that were going on when another event occurred.

    EXAMPLES   I **was watching** television when the phone rang.

                      *Je **regardais** la télé quand le téléphone a sonné.*

indefinite article (See **article.**)

indirect object An indirect object is a word or word group that tells *to whom* or *to what* or *for whom* or *for what* the action of the verb is done.

    EXAMPLES   The teacher gave **the students** their assignments.

                      *Le prof a donné les devoirs **aux étudiants.***

indirect object pronoun (See **pronoun.**)

interrogative adjective An interrogative adjective is an adjective that introduces a question.

    EXAMPLES   **Which** class do you like?

                      ***Quel** cours aimes-tu?*

interrogative pronoun An interrogative pronoun is a word that stands for a noun and introduces a question.

    EXAMPLES   **Which one** do you like?

                      ***Laquelle** aimes-tu?*

interrogative sentence An interrogative sentence asks a question and is followed by a question mark.

EXAMPLES   Are you coming with us?
*Tu viens avec nous***?**

irregular verb An irregular verb is a verb whose forms do not follow a regular, predictable pattern.

mood Mood is the form a verb takes to indicate the attitude of the speaker. (See also **imperative mood, conditional,** and **subjunctive mood.**)

noun A noun names a person, place, thing, or idea.

EXAMPLES   **Carol** brought the **music** to the **party.**
Carole *a apporté de la **musique** à la **boum.***

number Number is the form a word takes to indicate whether it is singular or plural.

EXAMPLES   The **children** ate some **cookies.**
Les enfants ont *mangé **des biscuits.***

partitive article (See **article.**)

placement Placement refers to the position of words in a sentence or phrase in relation to other words in the sentence or phrase.

possessive adjective A possessive adjective is an adjective that indicates to whom or what something belongs.

EXAMPLES   This is **my** pencil. These are **their** friends.
*C'est **mon** crayon. Ce sont **leurs** amis.*

preposition A preposition shows the relationship of a noun or a pronoun to another word in a sentence.

EXAMPLES   Michael is going **to** the swimming pool **with** Sophie.
*Michel va aller **à** la piscine **avec** Sophie.*

pronoun A pronoun is used in place of one or more nouns. (See also **demonstrative pronoun** and **interrogative pronoun.**)

EXAMPLES   Francine is going with her cousins. **She** likes **them** a lot.
Francine va avec ses cousins. **Elle les** aime beaucoup.

direct object pronoun A direct object pronoun is a pronoun that stands for the direct object of a sentence.

EXAMPLES   Do you like this dress? I like **it** a lot.
*Tu aimes cette robe? Je **l'**aime bien.*

indirect object pronoun An indirect object pronoun is a word that stands for the indirect object of a sentence.

EXAMPLES   Lisa sent **us** a letter.
*Lisette **nous** a envoyé une lettre.*

subject pronoun A subject pronoun stands for the person or thing that performs the action of the verb.

    EXAMPLES   **They** (Mary and Jean) are going to the mall.
                        ***Elles** (Marie et Jeanne) vont au centre commercial.*

reciprocal verb A reciprocal verb generally expresses *each other*. Because the action of reciprocal verbs takes place between two people or things, they are always plural. In English, we don't have recriprocal verbs—just reciprocal pronouns.

    EXAMPLES   Melinda and Robyn talk (**to each other**) on the phone often.
                        *Elles **se parlent** souvent au téléphone.*

reflexive verb A reflexive verb indicates that the action of the verb is done to, for, or by oneself. It is accompanied by a reflexive pronoun. In English, we do not have reflexive verbs, only reflexive pronouns.

    EXAMPLES   Let's **make ourselves** an ice cream sundae.
                        *Il se **brosse** les dents.*

regular verb A regular verb is a verb whose forms follow a regular, predictable pattern.

    EXAMPLES   Marie **likes** French.
                        *Marie **aime** le français.*

relative pronoun A relative pronoun is used to join two or more related ideas in a single sentence. They can be subjects, objects, or objects of prepositions, and they can refer to people or things.

    EXAMPLES   That's the boy **who** lives beside us.
                        *C'est le garçon **qui** habite à côté de chez nous.*

subject A subject is a word, phrase, or clause that performs the action of the verb.

    EXAMPLES   **Their children** are cute.
                        ***Leurs enfants** sont mignons.*

subject pronoun (See **pronoun.**)

subject-verb agreement (See **agreement.**)

subjunctive mood The subjunctive mood is used to express a suggestion, a necessity, a condition contrary to fact, or a wish.

    EXAMPLES   If I **were** you, I would tell the truth.
                        *Il faut **que tu dises** la vérité.*

tense The tense of verbs indicates the time of the action or state of being that is expressed by the verb.

    EXAMPLES   She **is singing.** She **sang.** She will **sing.**
                        *Elle **chante.** Elle **a chanté.** Elle **chantera.***

verb A verb expresses an action or a state of being. (See also **conditional, imperfect, irregular verb, reciprocal verb, reflexive verb,** and **regular verb.**)

    EXAMPLES   Lawrence **plays** basketball. She **is** French.
                        *Laurent **joue** au basket. Elle **est** française.*

Grammar of Allez, viens! French 1

CHAPITRE 1

■ **NEGATIVE STATEMENTS** *Allez, viens! Level 1, p. 26*

C H A P I T R E 1

> **In English** An affirmative statement can be contradicted or made negative by adding the word **not** or its contraction, such as **isn't** or **don't**. Compare the following sentences:
>
> | AFFIRMATIVE | NEGATIVE |
> |---|---|
> | They are French. | They are **not** French. |
> | She is reading a good book. | She **isn't** reading a good book. |
> | I like chocolate. | I **don't** like chocolate. |

A. Check the appropriate column to tell whether the English statements below are affirmative or negative. Underline any words that make the statements negative.

	AFFIRMATIVE	NEGATIVE
1. My sister is <u>not</u> going home until later.		✓
2. They are from San Francisco.		
3. I can't see well without my glasses.		
4. She doesn't like to play with dolls.		
5. I'm studying French and English.		
6. Our car wouldn't start this morning.		

> **In French** An affirmative statement can be made negative by placing **ne** in front of the verb and **pas** after it. Compare the following sentences:
>
> | AFFIRMATIVE | NEGATIVE |
> |---|---|
> | Je parle français. | Je **ne** parle **pas** français.. |
>
> When the verb begins with a vowel (or vowel sound), **ne** becomes **n'** and forms a contraction. In French, the use of **n'** before a vowel is not optional.
>
> | | |
> |---|---|
> | J'aime le chocolate. | Je **n'**aime **pas** le chocolate. |

B. Check the appropriate column to tell whether the French statements below are affirmative or negative. Underline any words that make the statements negative.

	AFFIRMATIVE	NEGATIVE
1. J'ai quatorze ans.	✓	
2. Elle n'aime pas les escargots.		
3. Thuy et Isabelle adorent le cinéma.		
4. Tu n'as pas douze ans.		

5. Nous n'aimons pas regarder la télévision. _____ _____

6. Eric aime bien voyager. _____ _____

C. Rewrite the following French sentences as negative statements.

1. J'aime les examens.

_____

2. Tu préfères la pizza.

_____

3. Sandrine aime danser.

_____

4. François adore le sport.

_____

5. Tu as onze ans.

_____

6. Vous aimez nager.

_____

7. Nous adorons la salade.

_____

D. How are negative statements in French and English similar? How do they differ?

Similarities: _____

_____

_____

Differences: _____

_____

_____

> **In English** A noun can be a person, a place, an object, an animal, or an idea. Often a noun is introduced by the definite article **the.**
>
> I went to **the** <u>party</u> with Paul. (*party* is a singular noun)
> She returned **the** <u>books</u> to Marion. (*books* is a plural noun)
> **The** <u>girl</u> ran a good race. (*girl* is a singular noun)
> I gave **the** <u>boys</u> some money for a snack. (*boys* is a plural noun)
>
> Just as we use **the** with both singular and plural nouns, we also use it both with nouns that are clearly masculine (like the word *boys)* and nouns that are clearly feminine (like the word *girl)*. Most nouns in English—words like *table, house,* or *cars*—are neither masculine nor feminine; that is, they have no gender.

A. Circle each definite article in the following English sentences and underline the noun that follows each article. Then check the appropriate boxes to tell whether each noun you underlined is singular (S) or plural (P) and whether it can be classified as masculine (M), feminine (F), or whether it has no gender.

1. They bought (the) <u>house</u> next door.

2. She made a chocolate cake for the boys.

3. The businessman is wearing a funny tie.

4. She put the new tools away.

5. The ship sailed to Martinique.

6. John painted the houses in one day.

7. The girls love the cat.

	S	P	M	F	no gender
1.	✓				✓

> **In French** There are four forms of the definite article: in French, **le, la, l',** and **les.** The form that is used depends on the gender (masculine or feminine) and the number (singular or plural) of the noun. While only some nouns in English have a gender, all French nouns are either masculine or feminine.
>
> Use **la** with feminine nouns: **la** <u>pizza</u>   **la** <u>glace</u>
>
> Use **le** with masculine nouns: **le** <u>chocolat</u>   **le** <u>sport</u>
>
> Use **l'** with any singular noun
> that begins with a vowel (or a
> vowel sound) whether they   **l'**<u>école</u> (*feminine*)   **l'**<u>escargot</u> (*masculine*)
> are masculine or feminine:
>
> Use **les** with all plural nouns
> whether they are masculine   **les** <u>écoles</u> (*feminine*)   **les** <u>escargots</u> (*masculine*)
> or feminine:

B. Circle the definite articles in the following French sentences, then underline the noun each article goes with. Check the appropriate boxes to tell whether each noun you underline is singular (S) or plural (P) and whether it is masculine (M) or feminine (F). (You may need to look some of the nouns up in your book to tell what gender they are.)

	S	P	M	F
	✓			✓

1. Sophie adore (la) <u>glace</u>.

2. Ils aiment bien le magasin.

3. Tu n'aimes pas les hamburgers?

4. Je préfère les frites.

5. Vous aimez l'anglais?

C. Complete the following French sentences with the correct definite article.

1. Tu aimes ___le___ football?

2. J'adore _____ vacances.

3. Moi aussi, j'aime _____ plage à Miami.

4. Tu aimes _____ école?

5. Jean n'aime pas _____ examens.

6. Etienne préfère _____ chocolat.

7. Tu aimes _____ escargots?

8. J'aime _____ français, mais je n'aime pas _____ anglais.

Compare Now, compare the following sentences:

J'aime **les** <u>frites</u>.   I like <u>French fries</u>.

Notice that in the English sentence, there is no definite article. We only need a definite article in English if we're talking about a specific thing. (I like **the** <u>French fries at that restaurant</u>.) In French, nouns are almost always preceded by an article. When you learn a new noun be sure to learn the gender too, so you can use the right article with it.

D. If the sentences in Activity C were in English, only one of them would contain a definite article. Which one? In what way is this sentence different from the others?

_____

_____

_____

_____

_____

In English Every sentence has a subject. You can tell who or what the subject is by asking yourself who is doing something or what is being described. The subject may be a noun or a pronoun. In the following sentences, the subject is highlighted:

The students like their new teacher. (noun)
Sam has a blue car. (proper noun)
I am fourteen. (pronoun)

Pronouns are words that stand for a noun or a proper noun. The subject pronouns in English are **I, you, he, she, it, we,** and **they.** Notice how the pronoun below is used to avoid repeating the subject once it has been made clear.

<u>Thomas</u> lives next door. **He** is from Louisiana.

A. Underline the subjects in each of the following sentences. Then look at the sentences again and circle the subjects that are pronouns.

1. (She) plays tennis every day.

2. The pilot landed the plane with ease.

3. The movers are carrying a grand piano.

4. You look great today!

5. Marie is seldom late.

6. We like pizza.

7. They're very happy.

In French The subject of a French sentence is also the person or thing that is doing something or is being described. Just as in English, it can be a proper name, a noun, or a pronoun.

Sophie aime le chocolat. (proper name)
Les amis adorent la pizza. (noun)
Il s'appelle Lucien. (pronoun)

French pronouns also stand for a noun or a proper noun. The subject pronouns in French are **je** or **j'** *(I)*, **tu** *(you)*, **il** *(he)*, **elle** *(she)*, **nous** *(we)*, **vous** *(you)*, **ils** *(they)*, and **elles** *(they)*.

To say *you*, use **tu** to talk to a friend or a family member. Use **vous** to talk to more than one person or an adult who is not a family member.

To say *they*, use **elles** when you are talking about two or more females. Use **ils** when talking about a group of males or when talking about a mixed group of males and females.

B. Underline the subjects of the following sentences. Then read the sentences again and circle the subject pronouns.

1. (Vous) aimez le français?

2. Lisette adore le sport.

3. Monsieur et Madame Hupert aiment le cinéma.

4. J'ai quatorze ans.

5. Nous aimons les escargots.

6. M. Roland n'aime pas faire du sport.

7. Elle adore le chocolat.

C. Underline the subjects in the following French sentences. Then write the subject pronoun that could replace each subject.

1. Nicole aime regarder la télé.   **Elle** _____

2. Philippe n'aime pas faire le ménage.   _____

3. Michèle et moi aimons nager.   _____

4. Jean préfère écouter de la musique.   _____

5. Danielle adore le français.   _____

6. M. et Mme Roland aiment nager.   _____

7. Claudette et Marie-Claire ont seize ans.   _____

8. Bruno et Robert aiment faire du ski.   _____

D. Look again at the subject pronouns you wrote in the last three items in Activity C. In your own words, explain why you chose each pronoun.

1. M. et Mme Roland:

_____

_____

2. Claudette et Marie Claire:

_____

_____

3. Bruno et Robert:

_____

_____

French 1 Allez, viens!, Chapter 1

In English Verbs are words that express actions or states of being. The endings of most present-tense verbs in English change only when the subject, or the doer of the action, is *he, she, it,* or a proper name like *Marion.* This is called subject-verb agreement. With these subjects, an **-s** is added at the end of the verb.

I	sing	we	sing
you	sing	you	sing
he, she, it	sings	they	sing

A. Underline the subjects in the following English sentences. Then go back and underline the verb that goes with each subject. Two of the verbs end in an **-s** because they go with a singular subject. Circle those two endings.

1. We ride our bikes to school sometimes.

2. Gary rides his bike to school, too.

3. Jeannette and Sandra like football.

4. Sandra likes school, too.

5. You and Peter go to the movies on Fridays.

6. I play sports after school.

In French French verb forms vary much more than English verb forms, but they follow predictable patterns. Once you learn the pattern of a group of verbs, you'll know how to form other verbs within that group. For example, if you know the forms of **aimer,** an **-er verb,** you can use hundreds of verbs that end in **-er.** Look at the endings of the verb forms for **aimer.**

j'aim**e**	nous aim**ons**
tu aim**es**	vous aim**ez**
il/elle aim**e**	ils/elle aim**ent**

To use any of the many other **-er** verbs like **aimer,** just take off the **-er** at the end of the verb, and add the ending you need. Make sure the ending is the one that goes with the subject of the sentence. For example, if je (or j') is the subject of the verb, the ending you add will be **-e.**

B. Underline the subject and the verb in the following French sentences. Then go back and circle the ending of each verb.

1. Tu aimes bien l'école?

2. Micheline adore les maths.

3. Les amis parlent au téléphone.

4. J'étudie les maths.

5. Nous adorons les vacances.

6. M. et Mme Blanchard, vous regardez la télé?

C. Complete the following sentences with the correct form the of the **-er** verb in parentheses.

1. Je _____ **nage** _____ (nager) surtout le week-end.

2. Ils _____ (regarder) la télé.

3. Tu _____ (écouter) de la musique classique?

4. Nous _____ (danser) très bien.

5. Paul et Sandrine, vous _____ (étudier) le français.

6. Mme Bertrand _____ (voyager) beaucoup.

7. Tu _____ (aimer) faire du sport?

8. Elles _____ (regarder) la télé.

9. Il _____ (parler) français.

D. In your own words, explain how you can figure out the forms of unfamiliar **-er** verbs. Use the verb **parler** as an example.

_____

_____

_____

_____

_____

_____

CHAPITRE 2

■ CONTRADICTING A NEGATIVE STATEMENT

In English Contradicting a negative statement or question means giving an affirmative response to a negative statement or question. In English, you can emphasize disagreement by changing the pitch of your voice or adding stress to important words.

> –You don't like spinach, do you?
> –<u>Yes</u>, I <u>do</u>.

A. In each of the following conversations, does the second sentence affirm or contradict the first sentence?

	AFFIRM	CONTRADICT
1. —Is he going to the store? —Yes, he is.	✓	
2. —She's not wearing a blue dress, is she? —Yes, she is.		
3. —They don't have the right answer. —Yes, they do.		
4. —The last day of school is June 1st. —Yes, it is.		
5. —We aren't going skiing? —Yes, we are.		
6. —She isn't going with him, is she? —Yes, she is.		

In French To contradict a negative statement or response, instead of changing the pitch of your voice or adding stress to certain words, you use the word **si** instead of **oui** in your response.

> –Tu n'aimes pas les maths?
> –**Si**, j'aime bien les maths.

B. Would you use **si** or **oui** to respond affirmatively to the following? (Remember: responding affirmatively to a negative statement or question means that you disagree with the statement and you want to contradict it.)

	SI	OUI
1. Tu as seize ans?		✓
2. Elle n'aime pas voyager?		

3. Il est huit heures. _____ _____

4. Vous n'aimez pas les escargots? _____ _____

5. Nous avons histoire à neuf heures. _____ _____

6. Nous n'avons pas chimie à onze heures? _____ _____

C. Write affirmative responses to the following statements or questions.

1. Vous aimez le sport?

Oui, j'aime le sport. _____

2. Mélanie n'aime pas les sciences?

_____

3. Tu n'as pas chimie ce matin?

_____

4. Thuy adore l'anglais.

_____

5. Michel et Suzanne n'ont pas espagnol.

_____

6. Elle n'aime pas voyager.

_____

D. Write a conversation in which two students discuss a third friend's course schedule and the classes he or she likes. They agree about some things, but disagree about others. Use both **si** and **oui** in your dialogue.

_____

_____

_____

_____

E. How do you contradict a negative statement in English? _____

_____

In French? _____

_____

How is it different in the two languages? _____

_____

_____

_____

In English A regular verb follows a predictable pattern. In the present tense, you generally add an **-s** to form the third person singular of the verb. Otherwise, the verb forms remain the same.

Irregular verbs do not follow this pattern and their forms may vary widely. Compare the following.

REGULAR	IRREGULAR
I **want** a pizza.	I **am** sleepy.
You **want** a sandwich.	We **are** athletic.
She **wants** some soup.	It **is** fascinating.

A. Underline the verbs in the following sentences. Are they regular or irregular?

	REGULAR	IRREGULAR
1. We <u>play</u> in the school band.	✓	
2. She is a good girl.		
3. I have a black and white rabbit.		
4. You go to the store on Tuesdays.		
5. Her father always bakes cookies.		
6. They rest after the game.		
7. Sandy loves pizza.		
8. They are very tired.		

In French Most verbs follow a regular pattern. The ending is removed and the appropriate ending is added based on the subject. Some verbs are irregular because they do not follow this pattern.

REGULAR	IRREGULAR
j'aim**e**	j'**ai**
tu aim**es**	tu **as**
elle aim**e**	elle **a**
nous aim**ons**	nous **avons**
vous aim**ez**	vous **avez**
ils aim**ent**	ils **ont**

C H A P I T R E 2

B. Underline the verbs in the following sentences. Are they regular or irregular?

	REGULAR	IRREGULAR
1. J'<u>adore</u> le sport.	✓	
2. Tu as quels cours aujourd'hui?		
3. Vous parlez au téléphone.		
4. Nous aimons surtout le chocolat.		
5. Ils regardent la télévision.		
6. Elle a chimie maintenant.		
7. Lucie étudie le français.		
8. Eugène et Carole ont allemand.		

C. Complete the following sentences with the correct form of the verb in parentheses.

1. Le matin, tu _____as_____ (avoir) quoi?

2. Céline _____ (aimer) la chimie et les maths.

3. Eric _____ (avoir) arts plastiques le lundi et le mercredi.

4. Nous _____ (adorer) chanter dans la chorale.

5. Vous _____ (avoir) sport cet après-midi?

6. J'_____ (avoir) étude le mardi et le jeudi.

7. Nous _____ (aimer) bien la pizza.

D. Compare the verbs in the chart above. In your own words, explain how regular **-er** verbs differ from irregular verbs, such as **avoir.**

_____

_____

_____

_____

_____

_____

CHAPITRE 3

■ INDEFINITE ARTICLES

Allez, viens! Level 1, p. 81

In English Unlike definite articles, indefinite articles are used to introduce underlined unspecified nouns. The indefinite articles in English are **a** and **an**. The article **a** is used to introduce nouns beginning with a consonant or consonant sound, and **an** is used to introduce nouns beginning with a vowel or vowel sound.

I need **a** backpack for school.　　Julie brings **an** eraser to class.

Adjectives such as *some, few,* or *several* can be used to introduce plural, unspecified nouns.

I need *some* books.　　Julie needs a *few* erasers.

A. Underline the articles in the following sentences. Check the appropriate column to tell whether they are definite or indefinite articles.

	DEFINITE	INDEFINITE
1. I brought in the plants last night.	✓	
2. Lucy is carrying a heavy suitcase.		
3. You don't have the herbal shampoo?		
4. The test wasn't very hard.		
5. An ant just crawled onto my foot.		
6. Did you mail a card to Aunt Ruthie?		
7. Did you give the book to John?		

In French The French indefinite articles are **un, une,** and **des.** While the use of **a** or **an** in English is determined by whether the noun that follows begins with a vowel or a consonant sound, in French, the indefinite article used is determined by the gender of the noun and whether it is singular or plural.

Use **une** with feminine singular nouns and **un** with masculine singular nouns.

une montre (feminine)　　**un** roman (masculine)

Use **des** with plural nouns whether they are masculine or feminine.

des baskets (feminine and plural)　　**des** ordinateurs (masculine and plural)

In negative sentences, use **de** (or **d'** before a vowel or vowel sound) instead of **un, une,** or **des.** Compare the following sentences.

J'ai **un** stylo.　→ Je n'ai pas **de** stylo.
J'ai **une** calculatrice.　→ Je n'ai pas **de** calculatrice.
J'ai **des** feuilles de papier.　→ Je n'ai pas **de** feuilles de papier.

CHAPITRE 3

French 1 Allez, viens!, Chapter 3　　Grammar Tutor **13**

Copyright © by Holt, Rinehart and Winston. All rights reserved.

B. Underline the indefinite articles in the following sentences. Check the appropriate column to tell whether they are singular or plural and masculine or feminine.

	S	P	M	F
1. Vous avez <u>un</u> crayon rouge?	✓		✓	
2. C'est une règle?				
3. Elle a un sac noir.				
4. Nous avons des feuilles de papier.				
5. Jing-Yu a un ordinateur.				
6. Tu as une gomme?				
7. Il a une cassette?				
8. Nous n'avons pas de livres.				

C. Check the appropriate boxes to tell which indefinite article belongs in the following sentences.

	un	une	des	de	d'
1. Marie n'a pas ____ ordinateur.					✓
2. Il me faut ____ crayon noir.					
3. Tu as ____ baskets bleues?					
4. Je n'ai pas ____ sac à dos.					
5. Vous avez ____ trousse violette?					
6. J'ai ____ stylos rouges.					
7. Je n'ai pas ____ stylos rouges.					
8. Tu as ____ feuilles de papier?					

D. Write a simple sentence in French that contains a definite article.

_____

Rewrite the same sentence using an indefinite article.

_____

Explain the difference in meaning between the two sentences.

_____

_____

_____

_____

CHAPITRE 3

> **In English** Demonstrative adjectives point our people and things. They must agree in number with the nouns they describe.
>
> SINGULAR
> **this**   I like **this** <u>backpack</u>.
> **that**   I need **that** <u>pen</u>.
>
> PLURAL
> **these** Do you like **these** <u>notebooks</u>?
> **those** She wants **those** <u>pencils</u>.

A. Underline the demonstrative adjectives in the sentences below. Check the appropriate column to tell whether they are singular or plural.

	SINGULAR	PLURAL
1. <u>This</u> homework is not mine.	✓	
2. Did you make that pie?		
3. How did he guess those answers?		
4. These toys belong to Katie.		
5. I bought that little red car.		
6. Did you write these stories?		

> **In French** The singular demonstrative adjectives are **ce, cette,** and **cet.** All three of these words can mean *this* or *that*. Use **cette** with feminine singular nouns. Use **ce** with masculine singular nouns that begin with a consonant, and **cet** with masculine singular nouns that begin with a vowel or a vowel sound.
>
>   **cette** cassette (f.)   **ce** bracelet (m.)   **cet** ordinateur (m.)
>
> Use **ces** with plural nouns whether they are masculine or feminine and whether they begin with a consonant or a vowel sound. **Ces** can mean either *these* or *those*.
>
>   **ces** cassettes   **ces** ordinateurs
>
> In English, you can use *this* and *that* or *these* and *those* to distinguish between objects. To say *that* or *those* in French, add **-là** to the end of the noun.
>
>   Do you like *this* <u>watch</u> *(these* watches)?
>   Vous aimez **cette** <u>montre</u> (**ces** montres)?
>   I prefer *that* <u>watch</u> *(those* watches).
>   Je préfère **cette** <u>montre</u>**-là** (**ces** montres**-là**).

CHAPITRE 3

B. Underline the demonstrative adjectives in the sentences below. Check the appropriate columns to tell whether they are singular or plural and masculine or feminine.

	S	P	M	F
1.	✓		✓	
2.				
3.				
4.				
5.				
6.				

1. Elle aime bien <u>ce</u> stylo rouge.

2. Tu n'aimes pas cette cassette?

3. Nous préférons ces tee-shirts bleus.

4. Pauline adore ce disque compact.

5. Il n'achète pas ce short gris.

6. Vous aimez ces montres?

C. Complete the following sentences with the appropriate demonstrative adjectives.

1. Elle préfère _____ce_____ sac vert.

2. Tu n'aimes pas _____ hamburgers?

3. Il achète _____ cassette de Céline Dion?

4. Je voudrais _____ classeurs-là.

5. Lisette n'aime pas _____ stylos rouges.

6. Marc adore _____ ordinateur!

7. Je n'aime pas _____ trousse violette.

D. How do the articles affect the meanings of the following sentences? Explain the differences in your own words.

Il me faut **une** cassette.   Il me faut **la** cassette.   Il me faut **cette** cassette.

_____

_____

_____

_____

_____

CHAPITRE 3

> **In English** An adjective is a word that describes a noun or pronoun. The spelling of an adjective doesn't change when describing masculine and feminine nouns, or singular and plural nouns.
>
> The <u>test</u> was **difficult**.
> We met our **new** <u>neighbors</u> yesterday.
> I bought a pair of **black** <u>jeans</u>.

A. Underline the adjectives in the following sentences and circle the nouns they describe.

1. Donna has a <u>cute</u> (brother) with <u>big</u>, <u>blue</u> (eyes)

2. The huge locomotive made a loud noise.

3. Our server spilled icy beverages on the clean floor.

4. Does Estéban know the secret combination?

5. He reads a lot of exciting mysteries.

> **In French** The spelling of most adjectives changes according to the gender (masculine or feminine) and number (singular or plural) of the nouns they describe. Adjectives are usually places after the nouns they describe. Compare the adjectives in the following sentences:
>
> | | |
> |---|---|
> | **Masculine Singular** | J'ai un <u>crayon</u> **noir.** |
> | **Feminine Singular** | Tu as une <u>montre</u> **noire.** |
> | **Masculine Plural** | Elle a des <u>crayons</u> **noirs.** |
> | **Feminine Plural** | Il a des <u>montres</u> **noires.** |
>
> To make most adjectives feminine, you add an **e: une montre noire**
>
> To make most adjectives plural, you add an **s: des crayons noirs, des montres noires**
>
> If the adjective ends in an unaccented **e**, you do not have to add another **e: une montre rouge**
>
> Some adjectives do not change form, such as **orange** and **marron.**

C H A P I T R E 3

B. Underline the descriptive adjectives in the following sentences and circle the nouns they describe.

1. Vous aimez cette (calculatrice) grise?

2. Il me faut trois cahiers jaunes.

3. Sarah achète ces classeurs rouges.

4. J'aime mieux les stylos bleus.

5. C'est combien, ce portefeuille marron?

6. Ils ont des stylos rouges.

7. Il a une maison blanche.

C. Complete the items below using one item from each of the boxes below. Be sure to make the adjectives agree with the nouns they describe.

un   des
ces
d'
cet
une
cette
ce

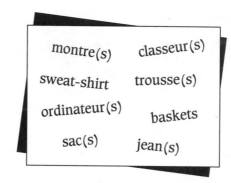
montre(s)   classeur(s)
sweat-shirt   trousse(s)
ordinateur(s)
baskets
sac(s)   jean(s)

gris
violet
vert
noir
rouge
jaune   blanc
bleu

1. Je voudrais ____une____ montre _____.

2. Tu as _____ _____ _____?

3. Mylène n'a pas _____ _____ _____.

4. Vous aimez _____ _____ _____?

5. Il adore _____ _____ _____.

6. Tu as _____ _____ _____?

D. Compare the French sentences in Activity B with the English sentences in Activity A. How is the placement of adjectives in the French sentences different from English?

_____

_____

_____

_____

_____

CHAPITRE 3

CHAPITRE 4

■ **QUESTION FORMATION**   *Allez, viens! Level 1, p. 115*

C H A P I T R E 4

In English You can change a statement into a yes-or-no question by adding **do, does,** or **did** to the beginning of the question. In some cases, you can change a statement into a yes-or-no question by reversing the order of the subject and verb or helping verb.

STATEMENTS	QUESTIONS
She rollerskates.	**Does** she rollerskate?
I like baseball.	**Do** you like baseball?
He is French.	**Is he** French?

In English, you can also ask a question by raising the pitch of your voice. Asking a question in this way can express surprise or doubt.

She's leaving for Paris.   She's leaving for Paris?

A. Rewrite the following statements as yes-or-no questions.

STATEMENT   QUESTION

1. You're going to lunch at noon.   **Are you going to lunch at noon?**

2. She likes ice skating and skiing.   _____

3. It's cold outside.   _____

4. They live in Miami, Florida.   _____

5. You will play tennis with me.   _____

6. She likes to go to the movies.   _____

In French You can change a statement into a yes-or-no question by raising the pitch (**intonation**) of your voice. You can also add **est-ce que** (or **est-ce qu'** before a vowel or a vowel sound) to the beginning of the sentence.

STATEMENTS
Tu fais du vélo.
Ils jouent aux cartes.

QUESTIONS
Tu fais du vélo?   **Est-ce que** tu fais du vélo?
Ils jouent aux cartes?   **Est-ce qu'**ils jouent aux cartes?

B. Rewrite the following statements as questions using **est-ce que.**

STATEMENT

QUESTION

1. Tu aimes nager.

Est-ce que tu aimes nager?

2. Hervé fait du patin.

_____

3. Lucie joue au golf.

_____

4. Ils voyagent à Paris.

_____

5. On fait de l'aérobic.

_____

6. Vous faites une promenade.

_____

7. Il pleut.

_____

8. Il fait froid en automne.

_____

C. How is question formation in French and English similar? How is it different?

Similarities: _____

_____

_____

_____

Differences: _____

_____

_____

_____

■ **THE VERB FAIRE** *Allez, viens! Level 1, p. 116*

C H A P I T R E 4

> **In English** To talk about sports and other activities in English, you can use a variety of verbs. Some of the most common verbs used in this context are **to play, to do, to make,** and **to go.**
>
> We **are going** fishing.
> He **is doing** the dishes.
> **Can** you **make** a cake for tomorrow?
> Steven **plays** chess.

A. Complete the following sentences with an appropriate verb.

1. Sam and Juan _____**are playing**_____ basketball.

2. My baby sister likes to _____ the hokie-pokie.

3. Tara _____ most of her clothes.

4. Do you _____ the piano?

5. When are we _____ swimming?

6. Doesn't his brother _____ minor league baseball?

> **In French** The verb **faire** can convey several different meanings. It can mean *to do, to make, to play,* or be used in certain expressions as an action verb. It can also be used to convey weather. Compare the meanings of the following sentences:
>
> | | |
> |---|---|
> | Nous **faisons** nos devoirs. | We *do/are doing* our homework. |
> | Ils **font** du sport. | They *play* sports. |
> | Tu **fais** un sandwich. | You're *making* a sandwich. |
> | Je **fais du ski.** | I *ski* / I *am skiing*. |
> | Il **fait** beau. | The weather is nice. |

B. Check the appropriate boxes to tell whether the verb **faire** best corresponds to *to do, to make, to play,* or an action verb. Write any action verbs in the space provided.

to do	to make	to play	action verb
			jog or go jogging

1. Vous faites du jogging?

2. Elles font du théâtre.

3. Qu'est-ce qu'on fait maintenant?

4. Il fait une pizza.

5. Nous faisons du sport.

6. Suzanne fait de la photo.

C. Complete the following paragraph with the correct forms of the verb **faire.**

Tu (1) _____**fais**_____ beaucoup de sport? Moi, j'adore (2) _____ du

sport. Je (3) _____ surtout du patin et de l'athlétisme. En hiver, mes amis et

moi, nous (4) _____ souvent du ski. Mes cousins Stéphane et Marc n'aiment

pas le sport. Ils (5) _____ de la vidéo et de la photo.

D. Compare the answers to the question below. What conclusion might you draw from these three very different responses about questions containing the verb **faire?** Illustrate your answer with two more responses to this question.

Qu'est-ce que tu **fais?**   Je **fais** de la natation.
Je **parle** au téléphone.
Je **fais** un sandwich.

_____

_____

_____

_____

_____

French 1 Allez, viens!, Chapter 4

ADVERBS

In English An adverb is a word or phrase that tells when, where, how, how much, how long, to what extent, or how often. Adverbs modify verbs or verb phrases, adjectives, or other adverbs.

The squirrels **quickly** gathered the nuts. (The adverb *quickly* modifies the verb *gathered;* it tells *how* the squirrels gathered.)
She goes to work **very** early. (The adverb *very* modifies the adverb *early.*)
The movie was **too** long. (The adverb *too* modifies the adjective *long.*)
We play tennis **every day.** (The adverb phrase *every day* modifies *play tennis;* it tells *how often* we play tennis.)

In English, the placement of adverbs is generally variable.

Quietly, he opened the door.
He opened the door **quietly.**
He **quietly** opened the door.

A. Underline the adverbs in the following sentences. Then, circle the word or words each one modifies.

1. She quietly tiptoed up the stairs.

2. You can truly imagine what life was like in the 1800s.

3. I always read the newspaper in the morning.

4. This sauce is too spicy.

5. Do you sometimes think about going to Europe?

6. He was really surprised about the party.

In French The placement of adverbs in French is not as variable as it is in English. Longer adverbs and adverb phrases may be placed either at the beginning or the end of a sentence.

D'habitude, je joue au tennis le samedi.
Je fais du ski **une fois par semaine.**

Short adverbs are usually placed after a verb they modify.

Je fais **souvent** du théâtre.

The negations, such as **ne... pas** and **ne... jamais** go around the verb.

Je **ne** joue **jamais** au basket.
Je **ne** fais **pas** de ski.

B. Underline the adverbs in the following sentences. Then, circle the word or words each one modifies.

1. Tu (joues) <u>quelquefois</u> au football?

2. Est-ce qu'il fait souvent froid?

3. Je parle rarement au téléphone.

4. D'habitude, nous faisons du camping.

5. Il ne neige jamais en été.

6. De temps en temps, Corinne fait du théâtre.

7. Ils font du jogging deux fois par semaine.

C. Write sentences using adverbs of frequency to tell how often you do the following things.

1. faire la vaisselle

   Je fais la vaisselle trois fois par semaine.

2. faire de l'aérobic

3. jouer au football

4. jouer au tennis

5. faire les devoirs

6. faire de la video

7. jouer aux cartes

D. Compare the placement of adverbs in the English sentences with their placement in the French sentences. In what ways is the placement similar? How is it different?

Similarities: _____

_____

_____

Differences: _____

_____

_____

CHAPITRE 5

> **In English** An imperative is a command, request, or strong suggestion to do (or not do) something. Commands are formed by using the infinitive form of the verb without the word *to*. Notice that no subject is stated in imperatives.
>
> **Go** to bed.
> **Do** the dishes, please.
> Here, **take** one!
> Please **don't wake** her **up!**

A. Decide whether each item is a statement **(S)**, a question **(Q)**, or an imperative **(I)**.

1. Are you going to eat that? __**Q**__

2. This is my little brother. _____

3. Have some pie. _____

4. Don't forget the milk! _____

5. May I help you? _____

6. Please pass the potatoes. _____

7. Is he watching television again? _____

8. Go to bed early. _____

> **In French** In French imperatives, the subject is also understood. Because French has two forms of *you*, **tu** and **vous,** it has two different ways of commanding someone to do something.
>
> | **tu** | | **vous** | |
> |---|---|---|---|
> | statement: | command: | statement: | command: |
> | **Tu regardes** la télévision. | **Regarde** la télévision! | **Vous regardez** la télévision. | **Regardez** la télévision! |
> | **Tu fais** tes devoirs. | **Fais** tes devoirs. | **Vous faites** vos devoirs. | **Faites** vos devoirs! |
>
> Use the **tu** form of the imperative with people you normally address as **tu,** such as friends, classmates, or family members. Remember, **tu** is not only informal, it is also singular. Use the **vous** form of the imperative when speaking to more than one person, even if they are a group of close friends or family. You also use the **vous** form of the imperative with anyone you normally address as **vous,** such as your teacher and other adults to whom you show respect. With **-er** verbs, you drop the final **s** when forming a command with **tu.**

B. Add the missing end punctuation to the following sentences. Add a period to statements, a question mark to questions, and an exclamation point to imperatives.

1. Ecoute ce CD __!__
2. Est-ce que tu as une montre _____
3. Donnez-moi un sandwich _____
4. Il est cinq heures _____
5. On va au café _____
6. Prends un steak-frites _____
7. Nous faisons une promenade _____
8. Allons au cinéma _____

C. Give a group of your friends some advice based on their comments below.

1. Nous avons un examen lundi.

   Etudiez!_____

2. Nous avons très soif.

   _____

3. Il fait du soleil.

   _____

4. Nous avons faim.

   _____

D. Now give your friend's little sister some advice based on her comments.

1. J'ai faim.

   Prends un sandwich._____

2. J'aime la musique.

   _____

3. Je voudrais faire du sport.

   _____

4. J'ai soif.

   _____

E. Look at the verbs in the second box. Which verb form changes when the statement becomes a command? How is it different?

_____

_____

French 1 Allez, viens!, Chapter 5

CHAPITRE 6

■ DAYS OF THE WEEK

In English To say that you regularly do something on a particular day of the week, you make the day plural (*Sundays*) or you can use an adjective, such as *every* (*every Sunday*). If you are talking about something that is going to happen on one specific day, you use the singular (*on Saturday*). Notice the difference in meaning between the following sentences:

Louise has a piano lesson on <u>Saturday</u>.
Louise has piano lessons on <u>Saturday**s**</u>.
Louise has piano lessons **every** <u>Saturday</u>.

A. Check the appropriate column to tell whether the following sentences refer to events that occur regularly or will occur on one specific day.

	REGULARLY	ONE SPECIFIC DAY
1. They leave for Hawaii on Wednesday.		✓
2. I do homework every Sunday.		
3. Marla goes swimming on Mondays.		
4. On Friday I have a doctor's appointment.		
5. You ride the bus on Thursdays.		
6. Her birthday party is on Saturday.		

In French If you want to say you do something regularly on a particular day of the week add **le** in front of the day and leave it singular. Compare the meanings of these sentences.

Nous allons au cinéma <u>samedi</u>.
We're going to the movies <u>Saturday</u>.

Nous allons au cinéma **le** <u>samedi</u>.
We go to the movies on <u>Saturdays</u>.

B. Check the appropriate column to tell whether the following sentences refer to events that occur regularly or will occur on one specific day.

	REGULARLY	ONE SPECIFIC DAY
1. Samedi, je joue au hockey.		✓
2. Elle va à la piscine le dimanche.		
3. Nous allons voir une pièce mercredi.		
4. Le mardi et le jeudi, on a informatique.		
5. Louise arrive lundi matin.		
6. Nous dînons au restaurant le vendredi.		

C. Write six sentences in French. In half of your sentences, tell something you do regularly on a particular day of the week. In the other sentences, tell what you are going to do on specific days this week.

1. **Le lundi, je vais au centre commercial.** _____

2. _____

3. _____

4. _____

5. **Vendredi, je vais aller au théâtre.** _____

6. _____

7. _____

8. _____

D. Compare the following two sentences. Besides the differences pointed out above, what other difference do you notice about days of the week?

We're going to the beach Saturday.   On va à la plage samedi.

_____

_____

_____

_____

_____

CHAPITRE 6

French 1 Allez, viens!, Chapter 6

> **In English** You can use the progressive form of the verb **to go** with the infinitive of another verb to talk about the near future.
>
> We **are going to eat** some ice cream.
>
> In this sentence, the verb phrase **are going** places the action of the sentence in the future. The action verb **to eat,** in its infinitive form, tells what you *are going to do.*
>
> Of course, you can also use the verb **to go** to tell where you are going. In such sentences, it is followed by a place rather than an infinitive of another verb.
>
> She **is going** to town on Wednesday.
> Sandra **is going** to the mall.

A. Do the following sentences imply near future, or simply tell where someone is going?

	NEAR FUTURE	WHERE
1. We're going to take a test on Friday.	✓	
2. Chris is going to take the train.		
3. They are going to the movies.		
4. Amy is going to sing in the choir.		
5. My mother is going to the gym.		

> **In French** You can use the verb **aller** with a place to tell where you're going.
>
> Je **vais** à l'école.
>
> You can also use **aller** with an infinitive to tell what you're going to do or what's going to happen.
>
> Je **vais acheter** un CD.
> Lisette **va faire du ski.**

B. Do the following sentences imply near future, or simply tell where someone is going?

	NEAR FUTURE	WHERE
1. Nous allons à la piscine.		✓
2. Mathilde va au musée.		
3. Ils vont faire une promenade.		
4. Vous allez jouer au football.		
5. Mes parents vont faire un pique-nique.		

C H A P I T R E 6

C. Underline the conjugated forms of **aller** in the following sentences. Then circle the infinitive phrases that accompany them.

1. Michèle ne <u>va</u> pas (prendre un coca.)

2. Tu vas avoir beaucoup de devoirs.

3. Ils vont aller au musée.

4. Vous allez faire les vitrines dimanche?

5. Nous allons regarder un film samedi.

6. Je vais jouer au tennis.

D. Write four sentences telling where you're going to go next week and what you will do.

1. **Je vais aller à l'école.** _____

2. _____

3. _____

4. _____

5. _____

E. Which of the sentences in Activity C is negative? What does this sentence tell you about the placement of **ne... pas** when talking about the near future?

_____

_____

_____

_____

In English A contraction is a shortened form of a word or groups of words. A contraction contains an apostrophe to show where letters have been left out.

Mom **isn't** going to like this.
She **wouldn't** want to go, would she?
I'm the only one here right now.

English contractions are commonly formed with the word **not** and forms of the verbs **to be, to do, to have, will,** and **can.** These contractions are not required. In fact, in formal writing, such as school papers or business letters, contractions may be inappropriate. Nevertheless, both of the following sentences are correct in the right circumstances.

I **do not** know.　　I **don't** know.

A. Underline the contractions in the following sentences.

1. You <u>shouldn't</u> just play all day.

2. He's going to be very pleased.

3. I've got a secret.

4. We don't know whether the story's true or not.

5. I can't tell if she's crying or laughing.

6. He doesn't understand the assignment.

In French The use of contractions in French is not optional, whether the situation is formal or informal. In some cases their purpose is to facilitate pronunciation. A contraction can make a sentence "flow" better by avoiding the placement of two vowel sounds together.

J'aime le football.

Other uses of French contractions are not related to pronunciation. Rather, some very particular circumstances call for the use of contractions. For example, the preposition **à** always forms a contraction when combined with the articles **le** or **les,** but **à** does not combine with **la** or **l'**.

Tu vas...　　**au** musée?
aux Etats-Unis?
à la piscine?
à l'école?

B. Underline the contractions in the following sentences. If there is no contraction, leave the sentence as it is.

1. Vous allez <u>au</u> stade?

2. Micheline ne va pas à l'université.

3. Mes amis parlent au téléphone.

4. Lucie aime jouer aux cartes.

5. Nous adorons aller à la plage.

6. Les élèves vont au centre commercial.

C. Tell where the following people are going by completing the sentences with the appropriate form of **à** plus **le, la, l', or les.**

1. Michèle va __à la__ piscine.

2. Je vais _____ musées.

3. Yvonne et Corinne vont _____ Maison des jeunes.

4. Vous allez _____ café.

5. Tu vas _____ école.

6. Nous allons _____ théâtre.

D. Underline the contractions in the following sentences. In what ways are they different?

Nous allons au cinéma.   J'adore le cinéma.

_____

_____

_____

_____

_____

CHAPITRE 6

In English Information questions differ from yes-or-no questions because they ask for specific information. You can recognize information questions by listening for question words.

Where is he going?
Why is the sky blue?
Who is at the door?
What are you doing?
When will the show start?
How are you feeling?

A. Underline the question words in the following sentences.

1. <u>What</u> is going on?

2. When does summer vacation begin?

3. Why doesn't she call me back?

4. What time is it?

5. How did you do that?

6. Who is at the door?

In French Information questions in French can also be recognized by their question words.

Quand est-ce que le train arrive?
Qu'est-ce que tu fais?

Unlike most English questions, in French the question word or words may be placed at the end of a sentence or the beginning.

A quelle heure est-ce qu'on va au stade?
On va au stade **à quelle heure?**

In conversational English, simple one-word questions are often used, but in French, such one-word questions sound abrupt and are incomplete. To make your questions convey a more complete idea, you can add the word **ça.** Compare the following short dialogues.

–I'm going to New York.　　　　–Je vais à New York.
–When?　　　　　　　　　　　–Quand ça?

CHAPITRE 6

B. Underline the question words in the following sentences.

1. Et demain, tu veux faire <u>quoi</u>?

2. Tu vas au zoo avec qui?

3. Quand est-ce que la bibliothèque ferme?

4. Qu'est-ce que tu veux faire?

5. Où est-ce qu'on va maintenant?

6. Le film commence à quelle heure?

7. Avec qui est-ce que tu vas au cinéma?

C. What question words are missing from the following conversation?

1. – On va au théâtre ce week-end. Tu veux aller avec nous?

   – _____?

   – Samedi soir.

2. – _____?

   – Au théâtre Molière.

3. – _____?

   – Avec Thomas et Sylvie.

   – Bon, d'accord. A samedi.

D. How is the response to the following question different from a short response to a similar question in English? Illustrate your answer with a sample English response.

–On prend le déjeuner à quelle heure?
–A onze heures et demie.

_____

_____

_____

_____

_____

_____

CHAPITRE 7

 **POSSESSION**

In English You can show that something belongs to someone by adding **'s** to a noun or a proper noun.

the **boy's** dinner   **Karen's** homework

You can show possession for regular plural nouns by adding an apostrophe to the end of the word.

our **dogs'** leash

You can also show possession in English by using **of.** The preposition **of** may be combined with *the* or with a possessive adjective.

the plays **of** Shakespeare
the strap **of** her purse

A. Underline the words that show possession in the following sentences.

1. Don't pull the <u>cat's</u> tail!

2. Is that Bob's cat?

3. That's our neighbors' newspaper.

4. Would you mind closing the principal's door?

5. The book's binding is cracked.

6. The teacher's book fell to the floor.

7. The hands of the clock are broken.

In French Unlike in English, in French, you do not use **'s** to show possession. You can show possession by using the preposition **de** *(of)*. With a proper noun, use **de** alone or use **d'** before a vowel or a vowel sound.

C'est le cousin **de** Stéphane.   Ce sont les parents **d'** Élisabeth.

To show possession with a noun, use **de** along with the noun and its definite article (**le, la, les,** or **l'**).

C'est la calculatrice **de l'** élève.
Voici le bracelet **de la** petite fille.

When **de** combines with **le** or **les,** a contraction is formed.

C'est le mari **du** professeur. (de + le professeur)
Ce sont les devoirs **des** étudiants. (de + les étudiants)

B. Underline the words that show possession in the following sentences.

1. Voilà le livre <u>du</u> professeur.

2. Elle aime bien la cousine de Philippe.

3. Tu as la montre d'Isabelle?

4. Ce sont les petits-enfants des voisins de Sophie.

5. C'est le chien de la fille de Maxime.

6. J'ai des livres du professor.

C. Complete the following sentences with the appropriate possessive words.

1. Voilà la montre _____**de**_____ Christine.

2. Vous avez les sacs _____ copines de Marc?

3. Ce sont les frères _____ père de Cédric.

4. Charlotte est la cousine _____ amie de Florence.

5. C'est la fenêtre _____ chambre de Christophe.

6. Ce sont les chiens _____ Eugène?

D. In your own words, explain how possession in French is similar to English. How is it different?

Similarities: _____

_____

_____

Differences: _____

_____

_____

■ **POSSESSIVE ADJECTIVES** *Allez, viens! Level 1, p. 205*

C H A P I T R E 7

In English Another way to show possession is by using possessive adjectives. In English, the possessive adjectives are **my, your, his, her, its, our,** and **their.**

my watch   **his** car   **their** books   **our** friends

A. Underline the possessive adjectives in the following sentences.

1. The Smiths bought their first house last month.

2. His hamster is sleeping in its nest.

3. Where did I put my keys?

4. You've finished your chores already?

5. It's great to hear that our soccer team won.

In French You can also show possession by using possessive adjectives. French possessive adjectives agree in gender (masculine or feminine) and in number (singular or plural) with the noun that is possessed.

	Masculine	Feminine	Plural
my	**mon**	**ma**	**mes**
your	**ton**	**ta**	**tes**
his/her/its	**son**	**sa**	**ses**

Notice the different ways to say **my** in the following sentences.

C'est **mon** cahier. (**Cahier** is masculine and singular.)
C'est **ma** tante. (**Tante** is feminine and singular.)
Ce sont **mes** parents. (**Parents** is plural.)

Use the masculine singular forms **mon, ton,** and **son** before feminine nouns that begin with a vowel or a vowel sound.

Voilà **mon** amie Sylvie.
Quelle est **ton** adresse?

The plural possessive adjectives also agree with the nouns they modify, but there are fewer forms. Notice that the masculine singular and feminine singular forms are the same.

	Singular	Plural
our	**notre**	**nos**
your	**votre**	**vos**
their	**leur**	**leurs**

B. Underline the possessive adjectives in the following sentences.

1. <u>Sa</u> sœur est très mignonne.

2. Leurs enfants sont pénibles.

3. Range ta chambre!

4. Votre fils a deux ans?

5. Nous faisons nos devoirs maintenant.

6. C'est une photo de ma grand-mère.

7. Il n'a pas son cahier.

C. Complete the following paragraph with the appropriate possessive adjectives.

Je vous présente _____**ma**_____ (my) famille. J'ai un frère. Je n'ai pas de sœur.

_____ (my) frère s'appelle Frédéric. Il a un chat. _____ (his) chat

s'appelle Lou-Lou. _____ (our) parents s'appellent Lucie et Georges. Ils ont deux

poissons rouges. _____ (their) poissons s'appellent Plif et Plouf. Et toi, tu as un

chien, n'est-ce pas? Comment s'appelle _____ (your) chien?

D. What are the possible meanings of the phrases below? In your own words, explain how the use of third person possessive adjectives in French is different from English.

son frère   sa sœur   ses cousins

_____

_____

_____

_____

_____

_____

CHAPITRE 8

▇ PARTITIVE AND INDEFINITE ARTICLES

Allez, viens! Level 1, p. 236

In English There are two types of nouns in English - count nouns and mass nouns. A count noun is something you can count, such as an apple or some books. When you use count nouns, you can refer to the whole item or to more than one of the item using the indefinite articles **a, an,** or the word **some.**

I would like **a** ham sandwich.
She borrowed **some** videos.

Notice that in some cases, you can refer to all of a count noun or to part of it.

I baked **a** pie.   They ate **some** pie.

A mass noun is something you wouldn't usually count, such as water, tea, or sugar, so you don't use **a** or **an** with it. Instead, you can refer to a part of or some of the item using the words **some, some of,** or **any.**

May I have **some** milk?   Do you have **any** flour?

In some cases, you don't need to use an article in English.

He's buying cookies, flour, and tomatoes.

A. Circle the nouns in the following sentences. Then, underline the the article or other word that describes the noun or tells "how much" or "how many".

1. Bring us some water please.

2. Does Casey have a car?

3. We don't have any milk.

4. She ate an apple and a sandwich.

5. Marie bought some grapes and a melon.

6. I'm afraid he doesn't have any money.

In French French also has both count nouns and mass nouns. You've already learned to refer to count nouns using the indefinite articles **un, une,** and **des.**

Je voudrais...   **un** avocat.
                   une pomme.
                   des oranges.

To refer to a part of or some of something, use a partitive article. In French, partitive articles match the gender of the object. Use **du** with masculine nouns and **de la** with feminine nouns. If a noun begins with a vowel or a vowel sound, use **de l'** whether it is feminine or masculine.

Je voudrais...   **du** gâteau. (masculine and singular)
                   de la glace. (feminine and singular)
                   de l'eau, s'il vous plaît.

Like indefinite articles, in a negative sentence partitive articles change to **de** or **d'** before a vowel or a vowel sound.

Nous n'avons pas **de** beurre.

Unlike in English, in French you cannot leave out the article.

Elle prend **du** yaourt.   She's having (some) yogurt.

B. Underline the articles in the following sentences. Then, tell whether they are partitive articles or indefinite articles.

	PARTITIVE	INDEFINITE
1. Je voudrais du pain, s'il vous plaît.	✓	
2. Vous avez des haricots verts?		
3. Il me faut un avocat.		
4. Tu ne prends pas de sucre?		
5. Prenez de la glace!		

C. Complete the following sentences with the appropriate indefinite or partitive articles.

1. Il me faut _____**des**_____ bananes et _____**du**_____ fromage.

2. Rapporte-moi _____ œufs, s'il vous plaît.

3. Ah zut! On n'a pas _____ lait.

4. Elle prend _____ pain avec _____ confiture.

5. Vous prenez _____ bœuf?

6. Je regrette, mais je n'ai pas _____ noix de coco.

7. Tu veux _____ pêche?

8. Dans la soupe, il y a _____ tomates, _____ poulet et _____ riz.

D. In your own words, explain the difference between the use of partitive articles and indefinite articles.

_____

_____

_____

_____

_____

French 1 Allez, viens!, Chapter 8

In English If the context provides enough information to make your meaning clear, you can use **some, any,** or a number without having to restate the noun . In English, you may drop the noun to avoid repetition.

> Do you want some eggs?
> Yes, I'd love some (eggs).

> Does Mrs. Thomas have any butter?
> No, she doesn't have any (butter).

> Do we have any onions?
> Yes, we have three (onions).

A. Answer the following questions without using the names of the foods mentioned.

1. Would you bring me some water? <u>**Yes, I'll bring you some.**</u>

2. Do you want some peas? _____

3. Did Kelly eat any dessert? _____

4. Do you have any papayas left?_____

5. Does Mr. Hanson want some salad? _____

6. Have the children had any milk today? _____

In French Unlike in English, to avoid repetition in French, you can't leave out the noun without replacing it with something. The pronoun **en** is used to replace the articles **du, de la, de l', des,** and **de** and the noun that follows.

The pronoun **en** goes before the verb. Notice how **en** is used to replace the noun in the second response to the following question.

> Tu as **de la confiture?**   Oui, j'ai **de la confiture.**
> Oui, j'**en** ai.

You can use the pronoun **en** with numbers and specific quantities of things.

> Il a un paquet <u>de beurre</u>. → Il **en** a un paquet.
> Ils ont deux <u>œufs</u>. → Ils **en** ont deux.

In a negative sentence, **en** goes before the verb, after **ne** or **n'**.

> Je n'**en** veux pas.

B. Underline the words in the following sentences that the pronoun **en** would replace. Draw an arrow to where the pronoun would go.

1. Vous ↓voulez du fromage.

2. Elle mange de la pizza.

3. Brigitte et Louise ont un kilo de pommes.

4. Le marché n'a pas de petits pois.

5. Pierre achète trois tartes.

6. Je veux de la farine.

7. Le serveur apporte une bouteille d'eau minérale.

C. Answer the following questions using the pronoun **en**.

1. Tu prends du pain?

   Oui, j'en prends.

2. Elle achète des produits laitiers?

3. Vous avez deux bouteilles de limonade?

4. Tu veux de la salade?

5. Tu as besoin des champignons?

6. Vous n'avez pas de sucre?

D. Explain what the pronoun **en** means in the following conversations.

1. –Vous voulez du jambon?
   –Oui, j'**en** veux une tranche.

2. –Vous avez des pommes de terre?
   –Non, nous n'**en** avons pas.

1. _____

2. _____

CHAPITRE 9

■ THE PAST TENSE

Allez, viens! Level 1, p. 277

In English There are several ways to talk about the what happened in the past in English. Compare the following sentences.

I **washed** the car.   I **have washed** the car.   I **did wash** the car.

Although regular verbs form their past by adding **-ed,** many English verbs have irregular past and past participle forms.

INFINITIVE	PAST	PAST PARTICIPLE
to do	**did**	(have/has) **done**
to go	**went**	(have/has) **gone**
to eat	**ate**	(have/has) **eaten**
to give	**gave**	(have/has) **given**

A. Underline the past tense verbs or verb phrases in the following sentences.

1. Carlos and Rita <u>ordered</u> soup and salad.

2. My grandmother worked at the grocery store.

3. The kitten hid inside the sack.

4. Her older brother drove to school.

5. Who brought the balloons?

6. We visited my grandmother many times.

7. She came to see us every Christmas.

In French To talk about the past in French, you can use the **passé composé.** The **passé composé** is made up of a helping verb and a past participle.

There are three types of regular verbs in French: those that end in **-er, -re,** and **-ir.** The past participle for each type follows a regular pattern. To form a past participle, change the **-er, -re,** or **-ir** ending of the infinitive as shown in the chart below:

TYPE OF VERB	INFINITIVE	PAST PARTICIPLE
-er verbs	**chant<u>er</u>**	**chant<u>é</u>**
-re verbs	**perd<u>re</u>**	**perd<u>u</u>**
-ir verbs	**dorm<u>ir</u>**	**dorm<u>i</u>**

The **passé composé** is not complete without its helping verb. In most cases, the helping verb is **avoir.** Notice that while the forms of **avoir** change to match the subject, the past participle remains the same.

J'**ai** mangé.   Nous **avons** mangé.
Tu **as** mangé.   Vous **avez** mangé.
Elle **a** mangé.   Elles **ont** mangé.

Like English, French also has some irregular past participles. Here are some past participles of irregular verbs you've already learned.

faire	**fait**	voir	**vu**
prendre	**pris**	lire	**lu**

C H A P I T R E   9

French 1 Allez, viens!, Chapter 9Grammar Tutor **43**

Copyright © by Holt, Rinehart and Winston. All rights reserved.

B. Underline the past participles in the following sentences and circle the helping verbs.

1. Qu'est-ce que tu (as) <u>fait</u> ce week-end?

2. Nous avons vu un film.

3. J'ai mangé de la pizza.

4. Claire a étudié à la bibliothèque.

5. Ils ont pris un taxi.

6. Vous avez gagné le match de hockey?

7. Les élèves ont visité le musée.

C. The sentences below tell what's going to happen in the near future. Rewrite them to say that each of the events occurred in the past.

1. Vous allez laver la voiture.

   Vous avez lavé la voiture.

2. Séverine va prendre le déjeuner au café.

   _____

3. Tu vas lire un bon livre.

   _____

4. Ils vont faire un pique-nique au parc.

   _____

5. Je ne vais pas parler au téléphone.

   _____

6. Nous allons manger la pizza.

   _____

D. Compare the following sentences. In your own words, explain how the placement of **ne... pas** is different in the past, present, and future.

PRESENT	NEAR FUTURE	PAST
Je ne prends pas le bus.	Je ne vais pas prendre le bus.	Je n'ai pas pris le bus.

_____

_____

_____

_____

_____

_____

_____

CHAPITRE 10

■ DIRECT OBJECTS

Allez, viens! Level 1, p. 309

In English A direct object is the person or thing in a sentence that receives the action of the verb. It answers the question *whom?* or *what?*

I gave him the book. (*The book* answers the question, "What did I give him?")
I introduced Peter to Mary. *(Peter* answers the question, "Whom did I introduce to Mary?")

Adjectives (including possessive adjectives and demonstrative adjectives) may also come between a verb and its direct object.

    subject verb adjective direct object   subject verb adjectives direct object
The library has interesting books.   They rode their new bicycles.

Compare the following sentences. In the second sentence, the preposition **to** comes between the verb **walks** and the object **school,** so **to school** is a prepositional phrase and not a direct object.

    subject verb   direct object   subject verb prepositional phrase
Scott walks the dog.   Scott walks to school.

A. Underline the direct objects in the following sentences.

1. The store also lends tapes.

2. Her parents drive an antique car.

3. Margie lit a candle.

4. I'm meeting George at the park.

5. Brandon studies French and Latin.

6. The dog always obeys his master.

7. She doesn't understand the lesson.

In French A direct object in French is also a noun that directly follows the verb without a preposition between it and the verb.

    subject   verb   direct object
Sophie cherche une robe.

Like English, adjectives, adverbs, and articles may come between a verb and its direct object.

    subject   verb adverb direct object   subject   verb adjective direct object
Patrice et Roland aiment bien le sport.   Lisette porte votre casquette.

B. Underline the direct objects in the following sentences.

1. Tu as ton <u>sac</u>?

2. Il apporte son manteau.

3. Vous prenez cette chemise?

4. J'ai mis une robe.

5. Delphine veut essayer ces bottes.

6. Philippe n'aime pas cette cravate.

7. Elles trouvent ces sandales un peu démodées.

C. Finish each of the following sentences with an appropriate direct object. Then circle the correct article or adjective that precedes it.

1. J'aime bien (le) la, les, l') _____ **chocolat** _____ .

2. Comment tu trouves (ce, cette, cet, ces) _____?

3. Nous avons pris (notre, nos) _____ .

4. Au magasin, Magali choisit (le, la, les, l') _____ .

5. Pour aller à une boum, Mireille met (son, sa, ses) _____ .

6. Tu vas acheter (ce, cette, cet, ces) _____?

D. Which of the following sentences has a direct object? Explain your choice.

J'aime le chocolat.   Je vais à l'école.

_____

_____

_____

_____

_____

French 1 Allez, viens!, Chapter 10

> **In English** Direct object pronouns refer to someone or something that receives the action of the verb.
>
> English object pronouns that stand for things are **it** and **them**. Object pronouns that can refer to people are **him, her, you, me, us,** and **them.** Direct object pronouns are placed after the verb.
>
> | | |
> |---|---|
> | Take <u>this package</u>. | Take **it.** |
> | She's calling <u>her parents</u>. | She's calling **them.** |
> | I want to invite <u>Billy</u>. | I want to invite **him.** |

A. What English pronoun would you use to stand for the underlined direct objects?

1. Finish <u>your homework</u> now.   _____**it**_____

2. My cousin found <u>his wallet</u>.   _____

3. Do you enjoy <u>books</u>?   _____

4. We don't like to do <u>the dishes</u>.   _____

5. The playful puppy bit <u>my finger</u>.   _____

6. They leave <u>their houses</u> at 8:00.   _____

7. She sees <u>her friends</u> every day.   _____

> **In French** The French direct object pronouns **le, la, les,** and **l'** can refer to people or things. **Le** can mean *it* or *him,* **la** can mean *it* or *her.* Use **l'** instead of **le** or **la** before a word that begins with a vowel or a vowel sound.
>
> | | |
> |---|---|
> | Il prend <u>la pizza</u>. | Il **la** prend. |
> | Vous prenez <u>ce pantalon</u>? | Vous **le** prenez? |
> | Tu aimes bien <u>mon frère</u>? | Tu **l'**aimes bien? |
>
> **Les** refers to people or things when they are plural. It does not change form before a vowel or a vowel sound.
>
> | | |
> |---|---|
> | J'adore <u>les frites</u>. | Je **les** adore. |
> | J'adore <u>les filles</u>. | |

B. What direct object pronouns would stand for the underlined words in the following sentences? If the form would change when placed where it belongs in the sentence, write both forms.

1. Vous achetez cette chemise?   **la; l' before acheter**

2. Je préfère le pantalon beige.   _____

3. Elle va essayer ces jupes.   _____

4. Nous aimons les hamburgers.   _____

5. Il prend son vélo.   _____

6. Tu n'aimes pas le fromage?   _____

C. Write answers to the following questions. Use an appropriate pronoun to avoid repeating the underlined words in each answer.

1. Tu aimes les escargots?

Non, je ne les aime pas.

2. Tu prends le bus pour aller à l'école?

_____

3. Tu n'aimes pas la chimie?

_____

4. Comment tu trouves cette robe?

_____

5. Tu n'as pas ton cardigan?

_____

6. Est-ce que vous préférez la robe blanche?

_____

D. Compare the following sentences.

Je **ne** le prends **pas.**   Je **ne** l'ai **pas** pris.   Je **ne** vais **pas** le prendre.

In your own words, explain the placement of **ne... pas** in sentences that contain direct object pronouns.

_____

_____

_____

_____

_____

_____

_____

CHAPITRE 11

■ PREPOSITIONS WITH GEOGRAPHICAL PLACE NAMES *Allez, viens! Level 1, p. 330*

> **In English** To say where you are going or where you are, you can use the prepositions **to** or **in** with the name of a city, state, or country.
>
> I live **in** Philadelphia.
> I'm going **to** Canada.

A. Complete the following sentences with either **to** or **in.**

1. Does he often go __to__ Rome?

2. Why don't we move _____ Texas?

3. I'll call you when I'm _____ Saint Louis.

4. My aunt resides _____ Arkansas.

5. Will they come _____ New England?

6. How often do you go _____ Ireland?

7. Her cousins live _____ Paris.

> **In French** When you say you're **in** or going **to** various geographical locations in French, the prepositions vary according to the kind of location you're referring to. Use the preposition **à** before the names of most cities. Notice that **à** can mean either **to** or **in,** depending on its context.
>
> Nous allons **à** Nice.
> Il est **à** Marseille.
>
> To say you're **in** or going **to** a country, you generally use **au** before masculine countries and **en** before feminine countries.
>
> Tu es **en** France.
> Elle va **au** Brésil.
>
> If the name of a country is plural, such as the United States, use the preposition **aux.**
>
> Nous allons **aux** Etats-Unis.

B. Underline the prepositions before geographical place names in the following sentences. Then, tell their meaning by circling either **to** or **in**.

1. Stéphane voudrait aller <u>au</u> Canada. (to) in

2. Tu as un frère qui habite à Londres? to in

3. Mes amis ont passé un week-end en Allemagne. to in

4. Je suis allé à la Martinique. to in

5. Nons prenons le train pour aller en Espagne. to in

6. A Paris, il y a beaucoup de musées. to in

7. Elle va aller au Brésil. to in

8. Son oncle habite aux Etats-Unis. to in

C. Complete the following sentences with **à, en, au,** or **aux.**

1. Charlotte est ___**aux**___ Etats-Unis.

2. Les élèves vont _____ Russie.

3. Qu'est-ce qu'on peut acheter _____ Maroc?

4. Lourdes habite _____ Mexique.

5. Nous allons passer une semaine _____ New York.

6. Je vais visiter les villages _____ Suisse et _____ Italie.

7. Magda a de la famille _____ Egypte.

8. Est-ce qu'il pleut souvent _____ Viêt-nam?

D. What do the feminine countries in the activity above have in common? Which masculine country also shares this feature?

_____

_____

_____

_____

CHAPITRE 12

■ THE PRONOUN Y

Allez, viens! Level 1, p. 367

> **In English** To avoid repeating a place name, you can say **there** instead.
>
> –Are you going <u>to New Orleans</u>?
> –Yes, I'm going **there.**
>
> In English, as long as your meaning is clear, you don't have to include the word *there.*
>
> –Is he at the doctor's office?
> –No, he's not.

A. Underline the word or words that the could be replaced with **there.**

1. Mom's <u>at the store</u>.

2. I can't wait to go to San Diego.

3. John and Julie are in Colorado.

4. Her best friend is moving to Seattle.

5. The State Fair takes place in Dallas.

6. They go to France often.

> **In French** The pronoun **y** can stand for a phrase that means **in, to,** or **at** a place.
>
> Mylène habite <u>à Bordeaux</u>.   Mylène **y** habite.
> Elle va <u>chez ses parents</u>.   Elle **y** va.
> Nous prenons un sandwich <u>au café</u>.   Nous **y** prenons un sandwich.
> Mes copains étudient <u>à la bibliothèque</u>.   Mes copains **y** étudient.
> Je suis allé <u>en Chine</u>.   J'**y** suis allé.
> Tu vas aller <u>aux Etats-Unis</u> demain?   Tu vas **y** aller demain?

B. Underline the words that could be replaced by the pronoun **y.**

1. Maman va au supermarché le lundi.

2. Est-ce qu'on peut aller à la piscine cet après-midi?

3. Laure fait de l'athlétisme au stade.

4. Didier et Thomas vont au cinéma avec Pauline et Marithé.

5. Cécile est allée à Berlin l'été dernier.

6. Tu vas au lycée le samedi matin?

7. Nons prenons le bus pour aller au centre commercial.

French 1 Allez, viens!, Chapter 12

Grammar Tutor **51**

Copyright © by Holt, Rinehart and Winston. All rights reserved.

C H A P I T R E 1 2

C. Rewrite the sentences above using the pronoun **y.** Be sure to put it in the correct place.

1. **Maman y va le lundi.**

2. _____

3. _____

4. _____

5. _____

6. _____

7. _____

D. Is the placement of the pronoun **y** similar to or different from the placement of other object pronouns? Use examples of sentences in the present, past and near future to illustrate your answer.

_____

_____

_____

_____

_____

_____

_____

_____

_____

_____

In English You already learned in Chapter 6 about using contractions. You may remember that a contraction is a shortened form of a word or a group of words. A contraction contains an apostrophe to show where letters have been left out.

I **do not** know the answer.   I **don't** know the answer.

In English, the spelling of a contraction can be irregular.

They **will not** leave before noon.   They **won't** leave before noon.

You may also recall that in English, contractions are optional, and in some situations they may be considered too informal.

A. What contractions could be used in the sentences below?

1. He does not know her.   _**doesn't**_

2. We cannot believe what happened.   _____

3. I am going to write him a letter.   _____

4. They are leaving in the morning.   _____

5. Mary is in the living room.   _____

6. He did not do his homework.   _____

In French You may recall that the preposition **de** often means **from** or **of**, but sometimes **de** is used when no preposition would be needed in English.

The park is near the post office.   Le parc est près **de** la poste.

When **de** is placed in front of a definite article (**le, la, les,** and **l'**), sometimes a contraction is formed. Unlike English, these contractions are required. Notice that there is no contraction of **de la** or **de l'**.

La maison est loin...
du musée.
des magasins.
de la piscine.
de l'école.

B. Underline the contractions with **de** in the following sentences. If there is no contraction, leave the sentence as it is.

1. Sur cette photo, Michèle est à côté <u>du</u> père de Sylvie.

2. La bibliothèque est en face de la gare.

3. C'est tout de suite à droite, devant le cinéma.

4. La pharmacie est loin du café.

5. Le Mexique est près des Etats-Unis.

6. La boulangerie est au coin de la rue.

C. Complete the following sentences with **du, de la, de l',** or **des.**

1. La banque est en face ____de la____ poste.

2. Le disquaire est près _____ café.

3. L'épicerie est à droite _____ bibliothèque.

4. La papetrie est à côté _____ cinéma.

5. La piscine est loin _____ magasins.

6. Le stade est à gauche _____ école.

7. La boulangerie est au coin _____ rue.

D. Compare the sentences below with those in the activity above. What conclusions can you draw about prepositions used in expressions that give a location?

Le jardin est derrière la maison.   La pâtisserie est entre l'épicerie et la librairie.

_____

_____

_____

_____

_____

Grammar of Allez, viens! French 2

CHAPITRE 1

■ INTERROGATIVE ADJECTIVES

> **In English** The interrogative adjectives in English are **which** and **what**
> They are both used to modify nouns.
>
> > **Which** play did they see?
> > **What** person told you that?
>
> Sometimes the verb *to be* intercedes between the word **what** and the noun it
> modifies. In this case, **what** is an interrogative pronoun.
>
> > **What** is the name of the store where she works?

A. Underline the interrogative adjective or pronoun in each of the following sentences.

1. What fell off the shelf?

2. What is the problem?

3. Which course is Lola taking?

4. What did Frank buy at the mall?

5. Which one is the best?

6. What is the address here?

> **In French** To ask which or what thing, use one of the forms of the interroga-
> tive adjective **quel** Like other French adjectives, the form of **quel** you use
> matches the gender (masculine or feminine) and number (singular or plural) of
> the noun it accompanies.
>
> | | SINGULAR | PLURAL |
> |---|---|---|
> | MASCULINE | quel | quels |
> | FEMININE | quelle | quelles |
>
> Because **quel** is an adjective, like English interrogative adjectives, it is accompa-
> nied by a noun.
>
> > **Quel** film est-ce que tu préfères?
>
> As in English, **quel** can also be followed by a form of the verb **être** *(to be)* and
> then the noun.
>
> > **Quel** est le numéro de téléphone de Sophie?

French 2 Allez, viens!, Chapter 1

Grammar Tutor **57**

B. Complete the following sentences with the correct form of **quel**.

1. _____**Quels**_____ magasins est-ce que tu aimes?

2. _____ sandwich est-ce qu'elle commande?

3. _____ sont ses couleurs préférées?

4. _____ est la date de ton anniversaire?

5. _____ chemise est-ce que Richard porte ce soir?

6. _____ musée est-ce que Lisette a visité?

7. _____ voiture est-ce que Céline va acheter?

8. _____ jean est-ce que tu prends?

Compare In French, **qu'est-ce que** also means *what,* but it is not an interrogative adjective. It is not followed by a form of the verb **être** and it means **what**. When deciding whether to use **qu'est-ce que** or a form of **quel**, you may find it helpful to write an answer to the question. In the following sentence, **qu'est-ce que** stands for the object of the sentence.

object
Qu'est-ce que tu aimes manger?   object
J'aime **la glace**.

C. Complete the following sentences with either **qu'est-ce que** or a form of **quel**.

1. _____ est ton sport préféré?

2. _____ vous faites?

D. Explain each of your choices in Activity C above.

1. _____

_____

_____

2. _____

_____

_____

CHAPITRE 2

■ ADJECTIVE PLACEMENT

> **In English** Adjectives in English are almost always placed before the nouns they modify.
>
> We heard a **beautiful** song.
> James is a **smart** boy.

A. Underline the adjectives in the following sentences and circle the nouns they modify.

1. Sandy bought a pretty green skirt.

2. My neighbor has a black dog.

3. Alex has never seen a foreign movie.

4. I'd like a nice, cold glass of water.

5. The first-grade students loved listening to fairy tales.

> **In French** Most French adjectives follow the nouns they modify.
>
> J'ai acheté un pull **rose**.
>
> A small number of French adjectives go before the nouns they modify. Since the adjectives that precede nouns are exceptions to the general rule, you'll need to memorize them. It may help you to remember them by categories. For example, the following adjectives refer to size, age, and beauty.
>
> | SIZE | AGE | BEAUTY |
> |------|-----|--------|
> | **grand** | **jeune** | **joli** |
> | **petit** | **vieux** | **beau** |
> | | **nouveau** | |
>
> Like other French adjectives, these adjectives agree in gender (masculine or feminine) and number (singular or plural) with the nouns they modify.
>
> | | SINGULAR | PLURAL |
> |-----------|------------------------|---------------------------|
> | MASCULINE | un **nouveau** vélo | de **nouveaux** vélos |
> | FEMININE | une **nouvelle** voiture | de **nouvelles** voitures |
>
> Notice that when a plural adjective precedes the noun, you use **de** instead of **des**.

B. Underline the adjectives in the following sentences and circle the nouns they modify.

1. Sophie a une (voiture) bleue.

2. Ils ont un chien méchant.

3. Les Morgan ont une grande maison.

4. La chanteuse a chanté une belle chanson.

5. Ma cousine aime les vieux films.

6. Christelle n'a pas de chaussures rouges.

C. Put the adjectives in parentheses in their correct places.

1. Monique préfère les _____ jeans ____**noirs**____. (noirs)

2. Nous avons une _____ voiture _____. (vieille)

3. Tu aimes leur _____ cassette _____? (nouvelle)

4. Le _____ garçon _____ a trouvé son chat. (petit)

5. Ma tante habite dans une _____ ville _____. (belle)

6. Je suis allé dans un _____ restaurant _____. (cher)

7. Tu as des _____ amis _____. (sympathiques)

D. Read the following three sentences. In your own words, explain the placement of the adjective(s) in each one.

1. Mon appartement a une cuisine moderne.

   _____

   _____

2. Mon appartement a une grande cuisine.

   _____

   _____

3. Mon appartement a une grande cuisine moderne.

   _____

   _____

◼ INDIRECT OBJECT PRONOUNS

In English Indirect object pronouns take the place of nouns that tell *to whom* or *for whom* an action is done.

> Lise and her mother made **them** crêpes.
> (The pronoun **them** tells us for whom Lise prepared the crêpes.)

You can ask yourself *to whom* or *for whom* the action occurs in order to determine what the indirect object is. Verbs such as **to send**, **to show**, and **to give** often have indirect objects.

> I sent **them** a thank you note.
> *To whom* did I send a thank you note? *To* **them**.

A. Underline the indirect objects in the following sentences.

1. Gabriel's friend showed <u>him</u> some other sights.

2. Did your dad teach you those magic tricks?

3. Let's write our congresswoman a letter.

4. Sam made us a table in shop class.

5. Save me a place in line.

In French Indirect object pronouns are also used to tell *to whom* or *for whom* an action is done.

> Je parle **à ma mère**.
> Le conducteur donne des billets **aux passagers**.

As in English, a sentence in French may contain both a direct and an indirect object.

> Carole donne <u>le cadeau</u> **à ses voisins**.

You can use a pronoun to avoid repeating the noun. If the indirect object is a person, you can use the pronoun **lui** (to/for him or to/for her); if it is more than one person, use **leur** (to/for them).

> Je **lui** parle.
> Carole **leur** donne le cadeau.

Notice that indirect object pronouns follow the same placement rules as direct object pronouns.

PRESENT	Tu **lui** offre des fleurs.
WITH AN INFINITIVE	Elle va **lui** offrir des fleurs.
COMMANDS	Offre-**lui** des fleurs!
	Ne **lui** offre pas de fleurs!

B. Underline the indirect objects in the following sentences.

1. Tu pourrais offrir un CD <u>à Sophie</u>.

2. Je dois téléphoner à mes parents.

3. Est-ce que vous pouvez donner un livre à Jean-Marc?

4. Le prof d'histoire va rendre les devoirs aux élèves.

5. Nous pouvons parler à Mylène et François.

6. Mon frère va donner une boîte de chocolats à sa copine.

7. Ma tante offre toujours des bonbons à mes parents.

C. Would you use **lui** or **leur** to replace the indirect objects in the sentences in Activity B above?

1. _____**lui**_____

2. _____

3. _____

4. _____

5. _____

6. _____

7. _____

D. Compare the following French and English sentences. How is the placement of indirect objects similar and different?

We gave the book **to the teacher.**   Nous parlons **au professeur**.
We gave **him** the book.   Nous **lui** parlons.

Similarities: _____

_____

_____

_____

Differences: _____

_____

_____

_____

CHAPITRE 3

CHAPITRE 4

■ RELATIVE PRONOUNS: CE QUI AND CE QUE

Pupil's Edition, p. 108

C H A P I T R E   4

In English You can combine or relate two ideas in a single sentence. For example, you could express the following in separate sentences or you could combine them using the word **what**. In this case, **what** stands for *something*.

I have to do something. I have to mow the lawn. → **What** I have to do is mow the lawn.

Notice that the relative pronoun **what** can function as both a subject or an object of a sentence.

SUBJECT	**What** bores me is mowing the lawn.
OBJECT	**What** I really like to do is play tennis.

A. In each of the following sentences, is **what** the subject or the object?

	SUBJECT	OBJECT

1. What she said was mean.

2. What happened to her was an accident.

3. What I'd like to know is what time it is.

4. What we have now is half of what we had before.

5. What caused the bright flash was lightning.

In French Two relative pronouns in French are **ce qui** and **ce que**. They both mean *what*. Like other pronouns, they stand for a noun or a group of words that serves as a noun. **Ce qui** stands for the subject of the clause it introduces. **Ce que** stands for the direct object. **Ce que** is usually followed by a noun or a pronoun that is the subject of the clause.

Ce qui me plaît, c'est de faire du deltaplane.
Ce que j'aime, c'est faire de la planche à voile.

Before a vowel or a vowel sound, **ce que** becomes **ce qu'**.

Notice that **ce que** is always followed by a subject, where **ce qui** is usually followed by a verb.

French 2 Allez, viens!, Chapter 4 Grammar Tutor **63**

Copyright © by Holt, Rinehart and Winston. All rights reserved.

B. Complete the following sentences with **ce qui**, **ce que**, or **ce qu'**.

1. _____ ils aiment, c'est faire de la plongée.

2. _____ m'ennuie, c'est d'aller à la pêche.

3. _____ Thomas préfère, c'est la pizza.

4. _____ les élèves n'aime pas, c'est les devoirs.

5. _____ mon frère déteste, c'est les petits pois.

6. _____ me plaît, c'est de déguster les fruits tropicaux.

7. _____ on va faire, c'est aller voir un film.

C. Fill in the first blank in each of the following sentences with either **ce qui** or **ce que**. Then, write a personalized ending for each one.

1. _____ j'aime, c'est _____.

2. _____ me plaît, c'est (de) _____.

3. _____ je préfère, c'est _____.

4. _____ m'amuse, c'est _____.

5. _____ je n'aime pas, c'est _____.

6. _____ m'ennuie, c'est (de) _____.

D. Compare the two sentences below. In your own words, explain the use of **ce qui** and **ce que** in each one.

1. Je fais **ce que** Maman dit.

_____

_____

_____

2. Thomas fait **ce qui** lui plaît.

_____

_____

_____

> **In English** Sometimes the action of a verb is directed (or reflected) back on the subject. These verbs may be followed by **reflexive pronouns** which include **myself**, **yourself**, **himself**, **herself**, **itself**, **themselves**, **ourselves**, and **yourselves**.
>
> I looked at **myself**.   He looks at **himself**.

A. Are the actions in the following sentences reflexive or non-reflexive?

1. He washed the car.

2. The dog scratched itself behind the ear.

3. Do you ever talk to yourself?

4. The speech was made by the President.

5. We enjoyed ourselves at the party.

6. She asked Anne where she left her keys.

REFLEXIVE	NON-REFLEXIVE
	✓

> **In French** Reflexive verbs are used when the same person performs and receives the action of the verb. The pronoun **se** used before the infinitive identifies the verb as reflexive (**se laver**, **se coucher**). Unlike English, French reflexive pronouns are placed before the verb. The reflexive pronoun changes according to the subject of the verb.
>
> Je **me lève**.   Nous **nous levons**.
> Tu **te lèves**.   Vous **vous levez**.
> Il/Elle/On **se lève**.   Ils/Elles **se lèvent**.
>
> Notice that some ideas in French are expressed with reflexive verbs, even though you would not need to use himself, herself, and so on to say the same thing in English.
>
> Elle **se lave**.   She is bathing.

B. Are the verbs in the following sentences reflexive or non-reflexive?

	REFLEXIVE	NON-REFLEXIVE
1.	✓	
2.		
3.		
4.		
5.		
6.		
7.		
8.		

1. Je me couche à 10h00.

2. Je vais à la piscine tous les jours.

3. Elle s'habille avant le petit-déjeuner.

4. Les élèves s'amusent bien le week-end.

5. Henri prend son dîner au restaurant.

6. Et ton prof, tu l'aimes bien?

7. Il faut se brosser les dents après les repas.

8. On se promène souvent dans le parc.

C. Complete the following sentences with the correct form of the reflexive verb in parentheses.

1. Ma cousine _____**se couche**_____ (se coucher) à 11h00.

2. Tu _____ (s'amuser) bien ce soir?

3. Nous _____ (se promener) dans les montagnes.

4. Gilles et Claire _____ (se lever) à 7h30.

5. On _____ (se baigner) tous les jours.

6. Vous _____ (s'ennuyer) chez vos grands-parents?

7. Combien de fois par jour est-ce qu'il _____ (se brosser) les dents?

8. Je _____ (se laver) le matin avant le petit-déjeuner.

D. Look at the chart of French reflexive verbs on page 65 again. Explain in your own words how you know which reflexive pronoun to use.

_____

_____

_____

_____

_____

French 2 Allez, viens!, Chapter 4

CHAPITRE 5

■ IRREGULAR PAST PARTICIPLES

> **In English** You may recall that in English, you can use either a verb in the simple past or a verb phrase made up of a helping verb and a past participle. You can recognize the second because it contains a form of the verb *have*.
>
> | BASE FORM | SIMPLE PAST | HELPING VERB + PAST PARTICIPLE |
> |-----------|-------------|--------------------------------|
> | start | start**ed** | have start**ed** |
> | ban | ban**ned** | have ban**ned** |
>
> For regular verbs, the simple past tense ends in **-d** or **-ed**. Past tense verb forms that do not follow this pattern are considered irregular. Below are some examples of irregular English verbs.
>
> | BASE FORM | SIMPLE PAST | HELPING VERB + PAST PARTICIPLE |
> |-----------|-------------|--------------------------------|
> | make | **made** | have **made** |
> | draw | **drew** | have **drawn** |
> | cut | **cut** | have **cut** |

A. Circle the verb form that correctly completes each of the following sentences.

1. We have just (began / begun) our project.

2. The lake (froze / frozen) hard enough for skating.

3. John and I have (knew / known) each other for years.

4. After everyone had (ate / eaten), we went for a walk.

5. Lena has never (drove / driven) before.

6. We (did / done) a science experiment in class today.

> **In French** You already know how to use the **passé composé** to tell what happened in the past. Similar to English, the **passé composé** is formed with a form of a helping verb (usually **avoir**) and a past participle. You may remember the three types of regular past participles in French:
>
> | | |
> |---|---|
> | **-er** verbs: | chanter → chant**é** |
> | **-re** verbs: | perdre → perd**u** |
> | **-ir** verbs: | choisir → chois**i** |
>
> All other forms of past participles are considered irregular. Below are some common irregular past participles.
>
> | | |
> |---|---|
> | être → **été** | voir → **vu** |
> | avoir → **eu** | lire → **lu** |
> | faire → **fait** | boire → **bu** |
> | prendre → **pris** | recevoir → **reçu** |
>
> In the sentences below, notice how the forms of the verb **avoir** change to agree with the subject, but the past participle stays the same.
>
> | | |
> |---|---|
> | J'**ai** lu. | Nous **avons** lu. |
> | Tu **as** lu. | Vous **avez** lu. |
> | Elle **a** lu. | Elles **ont** lu. |

B. Complete the following sentences with the correct form of the helping verb **avoir**.

1. Tu _____**as**_____ eu une mauvaise note?

2. J' _____ trouvé ma montre.

3. Ils _____ vu un joli appartement hier.

4. Michèle et Christine _____ fait la vaisselle.

5. Vous _____ reçu une lettre aujourd'hui.

6. Il n' _____ pas entendu la question.

7. Nous _____ lu ce livre en classe.

C. Complete the following sentences with the correct past participle of the verb in parentheses.

1. Joëlle et Jeanne ont _____**regardé**_____ (regarder) le télé.

2. J'ai _____ (prendre) le bus pour aller au match de football.

3. Ma meilleure amie a _____ (rencontrer) un garçon sympa.

4. Quel film est-ce qu'ils ont _____ (voir) hier soir?

5. Nous avons _____ (boire) de l'eau minérale.

6. Sandrine a _____ (être) collée aujourd'hui.

7. Vous avez _____ (faire) une promenade en ville?

D. Explain how to use **ne... pas** in the **passé composé**. Use the following sentence as an example: Il n'a pas joué au tennis.

_____

_____

_____

_____

_____

_____

CHAPITRE 6

■ THE PAST TENSE WITH ÊTRE

Pupil's Edition, p. 167

In English The past tense can be expressed with a helping verb and a past participle. This is similar to the **passé composé** in French. Unlike in French, the helping verb in English is always a form of the verb *have.*

> Stephanie **has married** our next-door neighbor.
> We **have visited** the museum of ancient history.

Also like French, English has some irregular past and past participle forms.

> He **spoke.**   He **has spoken.**
> We **ate** at the cafeteria.   We **have eaten** at the cafeteria.

A. Complete the following sentences with the helping verb **have** and the past participle of the verbs suggested.

1. admire   I _____ **have** _____ _____ **admired** _____ Mr. Collins for a long time.

2. drop   He _____ _____ _____ the ball.

3. wear   Bob _____ _____ _____ a tie to work.

4. sing   The choir _____ _____ _____ .

5. break   They _____ _____ _____ my vase.

In French You may remember that the helping verb in the **passé composé** is usually a form of **avoir.**

> Tu **as** pris le train?

A small number of French verbs use a form of **être** as a helping verb instead. When the helping verb is **être**, the past participle agrees with the subject. If the subject is masculine and singular, the past participle does not change.

> Je **suis allé** à une boum.

Add an **-e** to the past participle if the subject is feminine and singular.

> Catherine **est née** à San Diego.

If the subject is plural, add an **-s** to the past participle.

> Nous **sommes arrivés** à la gare.

If the subject is feminine and plural, add **-es.**

> Mes amies **sont restées** chez moi.

But, when the helping verb is **avoir**, the past participle stays the same.

> Luc **a vu** un accident.   Lucie **a vu** un accident.

French 2 Allez, viens!, Chapter 6

Grammar Tutor **69**

C H A P I T R E 6

Copyright © by Holt, Rinehart and Winston. All rights reserved.

B. Complete the following sentences with the correct helping verb (a form of **avoir** or **être**).

1. Tu _____es_____ rentré tard hier soir.

2. Nous _____ fait la cuisine.

3. Mes grands-parents _____ nés en 1940.

4. Elles _____ parties avant moi.

5. Tu n' _____ pas pris ton vélo?

6. Hélène _____ restée chez sa cousine.

7. Vous _____ visité le musée d'Orsay?

C. Write the correct endings of the past participles in the sentences below. If no change is needed, write an X in the space provided.

1. Thérèse est arrivé _e_ à 9h00.

2. Michel et moi, nous sommes monté____ au troisième étage.

3. Il est sorti____ de sa maison.

4. Ils ont pris____ le bus.

5. Mme Kléber, vous êtes descendu____ par l'escalier?

6. J'ai vu____ la nouvelle exposition au musée.

7. Elles sont retourné____ à New York dans l'après-midi.

D. Explain the agreement of the past participle with the subject of the sentence below:

Sandrine, Carole, Julie et Jérôme sont arrivés.

_____

_____

_____

_____

CHAPITRE 7

■ REFLEXIVE VERBS IN THE PAST

> **In English** The past tense of verbs that take a reflexive pronoun is similar to the past tense of other verbs.
>
> He **fixed** himself a sandwich.
>
> Like other English verbs, the helping verb is a form of *have*.
>
> We **have enjoyed** ourselves here.

A. What are the subject pronouns in the following sentences?

1. _____**She**_____ made herself a blue suit.

2. _____ have often asked themselves that question.

3. _____ heard ourselves on the radio.

4. _____ treated himself to a banana split.

5. _____ have already helped myself to some salad.

> **In French** The helping verb of reflexive verbs in the **passé composé** is always **être**. Like other verbs that use **être** as a helping verb, the past participle agrees in gender (masculine or feminine) and number (singular or plural) with the subject.
>
> Il **s'est coupé**.
> Elle **s'est coupée**.
> Ils **se sont coupés**.
> Elles **se sont coupées**.

B. What are the subjects of the following sentences?

1. __g__ s'est coupé.
2. ____ me suis baignée.
3. ____ t'es foulé la cheville.
4. ____ se sont bien amusées.
5. ____ nous sommes levés.
6. ____ se sont habillés.
7. ____ s'est couchée.

a. Nous
b. Frédéric et Marion
c. Joséphine
d. Elles
e. Je
f. Tu
g. Franck

C. Write original sentences using the reflexive verbs below to tell what you or your friends did and didn't do last week.

se casser   s'amuser   se promener   se lever
se brosser les dents   se faire mal   se coucher   s'habiller

1. _____
2. _____
3. _____
4. _____
5. _____
6. _____
7. _____
8. _____

D. Compare the two sentences below. Why does the past participle in the second sentence not agree with the subject?

Elle s'est lavée.   Elle s'est lavé les cheveux.

_____
_____
_____
_____

French 2 Allez, viens!, Chapter 7

In English To talk about sports and other activities in English, you often use the verbs *to do* or *to play,* or other more verbs such as *to make* or *to go.* In general, these verbs can be followed directly by the name of the activity.

Tara plays volleyball.   We do gymnastics.   My sister goes fishing.

To avoid repeating the name of a sport or activity, you can use the pronouns **it** or **them.**

Did you make your beds?   Yes, we made **them**.
Can he play his new guitar?   Yes, he can play **it**.

A. Replace the pronouns **it** and **them** in the sentences below with the names of specific activities. Rewrite each sentence in the space provided.

1. The children did them after dinner.

   The children did the dishes after dinner.

2. We played them.

   _____

3. They made it for her birthday.

   _____

4. Will you make them?

   _____

5. Can you play it?

   _____

In French To talk about most sports and activities in French, you use the verbs **faire** or **jouer**.

Je **fais** du ski.   Mon frère **joue** au basket.

The verb **jouer** is usually followed by **au, à la, à l'**, or **aux**. The verb **faire** is often followed by **du, de la, de l'**, or **des**.

If you want to use a pronoun to replace a phrase that begins with **du, de la, de l'**, or **des**, you can use the pronoun **en**.

Elle fait **du jogging**.   Elle **en** fait.

Like direct and indirect object pronouns, in the present tense, the pronoun **en** goes before the verb. In a negative sentence, **ne... pas** goes around the verb and the pronoun **en**.

Elle ne fait pas **de jogging**.   Elle **n'**en fait **pas**.

Remember that you use the pronouns **le, la, l'**, or **les** to replace direct objects.

J'adore **les** fruits.   Je **les** adore.

B. Replace the pronoun **en** in the sentences below with the names of specific things. Rewrite each sentence in the space provided.

1. Richard en fait tous les samedis.

   Richard fait de la planche à voile tous les samedis.

2. Nous en prenons souvent au petit-déjeuner.

   _____

3. Je n'en mange pas.

   _____

4. Elle n'en veut pas.

   _____

5. M. et Mme Chambord en achètent au marché.

   _____

C. Tell how often you do each of the following activities. Use pronouns in your responses.

quelquefois	rarement	de temps en temps	souvent	ne... jamais

1. Tu fais la vaisselle?

   _____

2. Tu fais de la gymnastique?

   _____

3. Tu fais de la musculation?

   _____

4. Tu fais la cuisine?

   _____

5. Tu fais des pompes?

   _____

6. Tu fais de l'équitation?

   _____

7. Tu fais les magasins?

   _____

8. Tu fais du patin?

   _____

D. The pronoun **en** could be used to replace a phrase in which of the following sentences? Explain your choice.

        a. Ils jouent aux cartes.   **b.** Elle joue du piano.

■ THE IMPERFECT

> **In English** The imperfect tense refers to actions or conditions in the past that were ongoing, that occurred regularly, or that were going on when another event occurred. In English, you say that an action or event occurred regularly in the past by using the words *used to* or *would.*
>
> During the week, she **would** get up at 7:00.
> My brother and I **used to** call each other often.
>
> You indicate that an action or condition was ongoing in the past by using a past tense form of *to be* (**was, were,** etc.) and a participle.
>
> I **was writing** my aunt a letter when she called.

A. Underline the verb phrases in each of the following sentences.

1. They <u>used to walk</u> to school together.

2. It was raining and the wind was blowing.

3. We used to spend every summer at the beach.

4. Sylvia was running late to her appointment.

5. Mrs. Brown would give us cookies after school.

6. Thirty minutes later, the food was getting cold.

> **In French** To tell what things were like or how they used to be, you use the imperfect tense.
>
> Jacques **avait** faim.   Jacques **was** hungry.
> Nous **étions** fatigués.   We **were** tired.
>
> You also use the imperfect to tell what used to happen in the past. Notice that in English you can express the same idea in several ways.
>
> I **would take** a nap every day.
> Je **faisais la sieste** tous les jours.   I **used to take** a nap every day.
> I **took** a nap every day.
>
> To form the stem of the imperfect tense, drop the **-ons** ending from the **nous** form of the verb in the present tense. The imperfect stems of regular **-er, -re,** and **-ir** verbs are as follows.
>
> | **chanter:** | **nous chantons** → | **chant-** |
> | **attendre:** | **nous attendons** → | **attend-** |
> | **choisir:** | **nous choisissons** → | **choisiss-** |

cont.

The imperfect stems of irregular verbs also come from the **nous** form of the verb in present tense.

avoir:	nous avons →	av-
aller:	nous allons →	all-
faire:	nous faisons →	fais-
prendre:	nous prenons →	pren-

Notice that the imperfect stem of the verb **être** is not based on the **nous** form.

être:	nous sommes	ét-

Add the following imperfect endings to the stem: **-ais, -ais, -ait, -ions, -iez,** and **-aient**.

B. Underline the verb phrases in each of the following sentences.

1. Nous faisions souvent du ski en hiver.

2. Tu promenais ton chien tous les jours?

3. Je prenais mon déjeuner à midi.

4. Mylène et Caroline avaient soif.

5. Vous étiez très fatigués.

6. Il faisait frais hier soir.

7. On allait toujours au cinéma le vendredi.

C. Complete the following sentences with the correct imperfect verb endings.

1. Je lis **ais**_____ des bandes dessinées.

2. Nous all_____ au supermarché le dimanche.

3. Bruno et Sylvie habit_____ à la campagne.

4. Tu promen_____ ton chien après l'école?

5. On av_____ très soif.

6. Ma sœur sort_____ la poubelle le vendredi.

D. Compare the verbs in the sentences below. In your own words, explain why their stems are different.

Je mangeais des légumes.   Nous mangions des légumes.

_____

_____

_____

_____

CHAPITRE 9

■ THE PAST TENSE: PASSÉ COMPOSÉ VS IMPARFAIT

Pupil's Edition, p. 265

> **In English** There are several ways to talk about the past in English. The following verb forms are usually used to tell what happened. They generally refer to completed events that occurred in the past.
>
> We **played** tennis.   We **did play** tennis.   We **have played** tennis.
>
> To talk about what was going on in the past or what used to happen, you use different verb forms. You can use *was* or *were* along with the -ing form of a verb or you can use the helping verb *used to*.
>
> We **were playing** tennis.   We **used to play** tennis.
>
> To describe people or things in the past, you can use *was* or *were* followed by a noun or an adjective.
>
> We **were** tennis players.   After playing tennis, she **was** tired.

A. Do the following sentences describe completed events in the past, or something that was a regularly-ongoing condition or activity in the past?

	COMPLETED EVENT	REGULARLY-ONGOING EVENT OR CONDITION
1. Brian went to the store, didn't he?	✓	
2. We used to have so much fun!		
3. Did you hear the phone ring?		
4. Joanie was watching TV last night.		
5. It was cold and rainy.		
6. I have finally made my decision.		

> **In French** To talk about the past in French, you need to understand when to use the **passé composé** and when to use the **imparfait**. Use the **passé composé** to tell what happened and to describe completed events in the past.
>
> Claire et moi, nous **avons pris** le bus.   On **est allés** au supermarché.
>
> Use the **imparfait** to talk about what used to happen or to describe people and things in the past.
>
> Il **neigeait** souvent.   Anaïs **avait** toujours froid.
>
> To tell what was going on when something else occurred, you can use both the **imparfait** and the **passé composé** together.
>
> Maurice **regardait** la télé quand nous **sommes arrivés**.
> Nous **faisions** la cuisine quand le téléphone **a sonné**.
>
> In both of the sentences above, the **imparfait** is used to tell what was going on, while the **passé composé** is used to tell what happened.

C
H
A
P
I
T
R
E

9

B. Do the following sentences describe completed events in the past or something that was a regular-ongoing condition or activity in the past?

	COMPLETED EVENT	REGULARLY-ONGOING EVENT OR CONDITION
		✓

1. Il faisait toujours beau le matin.

2. Jean était inquiet.

3. Je n'ai pas fait la vaisselle hier soir.

4. D'habitude, j'allais au café avec mes copains.

5. David a pris un café.

6. Odile a eu une bonne note en histoire.

7. Tu étais de mauvaise humeur cet après-midi.

C. Circle the verbs that correctly complete the following sentences.

1. D'abord, il (est allé / allais) chez ses grands-parents.

2. Soudain, j'(ai eu / avais) une bonne idée.

3. Il (a fait / faisait) toujours chaud en été.

4. Nous (avons pris / prenions) les bus tous les jours.

5. D'habitude, Patricia (est arrivée / arrivait) en retard.

6. Tout à coup, la voiture (est tombée / tombait) en panne.

7. Vous (êtes allé / alliez) souvent à la piscine?

8. De temps en temps, nous nous (sommes arrêtés / arrêtions) au parc.

D. Look again at the sentences in Activity C above. In your own words, explain how adverbs (words like **souvent** or **tout à coup**) can help you decide whether to use **passé composé** or **imparfait**.

_____

_____

_____

_____

_____

CHAPITRE 10

■ OBJECT PRONOUNS AND THEIR PLACEMENT

Pupil's Edition, pp. 288 and 293

In English An object receives the action of a verb. There are direct objects and indirect objects.

DIRECT OBJECT	Mr. Lee bought **a car**.
INDIRECT OBJECT	Mr. Lee bought **John** a car.

Of course, nouns can be replaced by pronouns. The object pronouns used to refer to people or things in the third person are *him, her, it,* and *them*.

DIRECT OBJECT	Mr. Lee bought **it**.
INDIRECT OBJECT	Mr. Lee bought **him** a car.

The other object pronouns refer to either the first or second person. They are *me, you,* and *us*. Their forms are the same no matter what type of objects they are.

DIRECT OBJECT	Mr. Lee called **us**.
INDIRECT OBJECT	Mr. Lee bought **me** a car.

A. Underline the object pronouns in the following sentences.

1. Would you like the band to play a song for you?

2. We never did bring you any flowers.

3. He called me last evening.

In French You may remember the pronouns that stand for things or people in the third person.

	SINGULAR	PLURAL
DIRECT OBJECTS	**le, la, l'**	**les**
INDIRECT OBJECTS	**lui**	**leur**

The object pronouns that refer to the first person and second person in French are as follows.

	SINGULAR	PLURAL
FIRST PERSON	**me**	**nous**
SECOND PERSON	**te** or **vous**	**vous**

These first and second person object pronouns are the same whether they stand for direct or indirect objects.

INDIRECT OBJECT	Tu **me** parles?
DIRECT OBJECT	Tu **me** comprends?

Before a vowel or a vowel sound, **me** and **te** change to **m'** and **t'**.

Tu **m'**écoutes?   Oui, je **t'**écoute.

Object pronouns are normally placed before the verb. When there is an infinitive after a conjugated verb, the pronoun is placed before the infinitive. In an affirmative command, **me** and **te** change to **moi** and **toi**. They are connected by a hyphen and placed after the verb.

Ecoute-**moi**!

French 2 Allez, viens!, Chapter 10

Grammar Tutor **79**

B. Underline the object pronouns in the following sentences.

1. Elle l'a vu au restaurant.

5. Tu ne veux pas me parler?

2. Tu leur as parlé?

6. Je te présente mon père.

3. Je vous invite chez moi ce soir.

7. Il nous a demandé pardon.

4. Excusez-moi!

C. Write answers to the following questions using pronouns to refer to the underlined words.

1. Il va voir ses cousins cet été?

Oui, **il va les voir cet été.** _____.

2. Tu peux m'aider à faire la vaisselle?

Oui, _____.

3. Tu as invité Michel et moi chez toi ce week-end?

Non, _____.

4. Vous ne voudriez pas nous acheter ce disque compact?

Non, _____.

5. Tu as donné un cadeau à Victor pour son anniversaire?

Oui, _____.

6. Je peux te parler?

Oui, _____.

7. Nous allons téléphoner à nos grands-parents?

Oui, _____.

D. In the following sentences, why do the past participles agree or not agree with the objects?

1. Mes amis? Je les ai invités à ma boum.

_____

_____

2. Ma soeur? Je l'ai vue hier.

_____

_____

3. Ma cousine? Je lui ai parlé ce matin.

_____

_____

CHAPITRE 11

■ IDENTIFYING AND DESCRIBING PEOPLE

Pupil's Edition, p. 315

In English To describe someone in English, you can begin by saying *he is* or *she is.* Your description may tell what a person is like or it may include other information, such as the person's nationality or profession. Both *he is* and *she is* can be followed directly by an adjective.

He is athletic.　　She is outgoing.

When *he is* and *she is* are followed by a noun, you use the articles *a, an,* or *the* before the noun.

She is an engineer.　　He is the president.

When *he is* and *she is* are followed by an adjective and a noun, you generally use the indefinite articles *a* or *an.*

He is a good driver.　　She is an artistic person.

Some nationalities can be both nouns or adjectives. If there is an article, the nationality is a noun. Without the article, it is an adjective.

She is Australian.　　He is an American.

Other nationalities have different adjective and noun forms.

She is English.　　He is an Englishman.

A. Do the following sentences need articles to be complete? If so, write **a, an,** or **the** in the space provided. If no article is needed, put an X in the blank.

1. She is ___X___ interesting.

2. He is _____ helpful neighbor.

3. She is _____ Swiss tour guide.

4. He is _____ astronaut.

5. She is _____ talented musician.

6. He is _____ French.

In French You can describe someone in French using **il est, elle est,** or **c'est.** **Il est** means *he is.* **Elle est** means *she is.* **C'est** can mean either *he is* or *she is.*

To tell someone's profession, use **il est** or **elle est** along with a noun. To tell someone's nationality, use **il est** or **elle est** along with an adjective. Like English, you do not use a definite article before an adjective. Unlike English, in this situation, you do not use an article before the profession.

Il est professeur.　　Elle est française.

You can also tell a person's nationality or profession using **c'est.** In this case, **c'est** is followed by a definite article and a noun.

C'est un professeur.　　C'est une Française.

If you describe a person with a noun and an adjective, use **c'est** followed by an indefinite article.

C'est un professeur français.

French 2 Allez, viens!, Chapter 11

Grammar Tutor **81**

Copyright © by Holt, Rinehart and Winston. All rights reserved.

CHAPITRE 11

B. Do the following sentences need indefinite articles to be complete? If so, write **un** or **une** in the space provided. If no article is needed, put an X in the blank.

1. C'est ___une___ chanteuse.

2. Il est _____ américain.

3. Elle est _____ professeur.

4. C'est _____ bonne musicienne.

5. Il est _____ antillais.

6. Elle est _____ canadienne.

7. C'est _____ Français.

C. Complete the following sentences with **c'est, il est,** or **elle est.**

1. ___C'est___ un groupe français.

2. _____ américaine.

3. _____ un bon professeur.

4. _____ acteur.

5. _____ une Française.

6. _____ chanteur.

7. _____ italienne.

8. _____ un Canadien.

D. Compare the two sentences below. What are two clues that tell you which nationality is a noun and which is an adjective? Explain your answers.

1. C'est un Anglais. _____

_____

2. Il est anglais. _____

_____

French 2 Allez, viens!, Chapter 11

CHAPITRE 11

In English Relative pronouns are words like *that, which, who,* or *whom.* Relative pronouns are used to refer to something or someone you've already mentioned.

That's the dog **that** bit me.
He's the new student **who** joined the hockey team.

You can use relative pronouns to avoid using two short, choppy sentences. Notice how a relative pronoun can combine two pieces of information about a single topic into one sentence.

They liked the song. I sang the song. → They liked the song **that** I sang.

Relative pronouns can be the subject of a clause or a direct object. **Who** and **whom** refer to people.

subject   object

Joe is the tennis player **who** won the match.   Sylvia is someone **whom** I admire.

That and **which** usually refer to things.

They played in the snow, **which** had begun to melt.   This is the book **that** I read.

In English, you can sometimes leave out the relative pronoun.

This is the book I read.

A. Underline the relative pronouns in the following sentences. Tell whether each one is a subject or a direct object.

	SUBJECT	DIRECT OBJECT
1.		✓
2.		
3.		
4.		
5.		

1. Linda is a friend <u>whom</u> I trust.

2. Billy read from a book that he wrote.

3. Mrs. Franklin gave me a toy that glows in the dark.

4. The lightbulb which had been flickering finally burned out.

5. That was a movie that we really enjoyed.

In French Relative pronouns in French serve the same purpose as they do in English. They can stand for someone or something that has been previously mentioned. Like in English, they can be a subject or an object within a clause.

Qui stands for the subject of a clause and is followed by a verb. It can represent a person or a thing.

C'est une fille **qui** parle espagnol.   C'est une chanson **qui** est célèbre.

Que stands for the direct object of a clause and is followed by a noun and a verb. Like **qui**, it can represent people or things. **Que** becomes **qu'** before a vowel or a vowel sound.

C'est une fille **que** je connais.   C'est une chanson **qu'il** aime beaucoup.

B. Underline the relative pronouns in the following sentences. Tell whether each one is a subject or a direct object and whether it refers to a person or a thing.

	Subject	Direct Object	Person	Thing
1.		✓		✓
2.				
3.				
4.				
5.				
6.				
7.				

1. C'est un film <u>que</u> je n'aime pas.

2. Louise est une amie qui est sincère.

3. Voici l'arbre qui est tombé sur notre maison.

4. La pièce que vous avez vue était bonne?

5. Francis est un homme qui est devenu architecte.

6. C'est l'histoire d'une fille qui habite à Nice.

7. Jocelyne est la dame que j'ai connue à Marseille.

C. Complete the following sentences with **qui, que,** or **qu'.**

1. La chanson _____**qu'**_____ il a chantée est très belle.

2. C'est une histoire _____ finit bien.

3. Le musée _____ nous avons visité était intéressant.

4. Christophe et Cécile sont les copains _____ j'ai rencontrés au centre commercial.

5. Il s'agit de deux jeunes filles _____ vont à Québec.

6. Maman parle à un monsieur _____ a fait le tour du monde.

7. Nous aimons les professeurs _____ ne donnent pas trop de devoirs.

8. M. Drillon est le professeur _____ mon frère préfère.

D. Read the sentence below. Why does the past participle (**faites**) end in **-es**?

Voilà les tartes que j'ai faites.

_____

_____

_____

_____

_____

CHAPITRE 12

■ **ADVERBS WITH THE PAST TENSE**

Pupil's Edition, p. 359

In English You may remember that there are several ways of describing conditions and events in the past in English. You can tell about events that happened only once or events that occurred regularly, you can describe conditions that occurred suddenly, or you can tell what things were like in general over a period of time.

Adverbs and adverbial expressions are used to signal when and how often conditions or events occurred.

SPECIFIC EVENT	REGULAR EVENTS-ONGOING CONDITIONS
once suddenly one day	often usually on Thursdays from time to time

A. Underline the adverbs and adverbial expressions in the following sentences. Do these sentences describe a completed event or a regularly occurring event or condition in the past?

	COMPLETED EVENT	REGULARLY OCCURRING EVENT OR CONDITION
1.	✓	
2.		
3.		
4.		
5.		
6.		

1. Laura went to the store <u>yesterday</u>.

2. Suddenly, the phone rang.

3. It usually rained when I washed my car.

4. I once caught a fish.

5. One day, a letter arrived from my cousin.

6. The choir often sang at weddings.

In French As you know, to talk about completed events that occurred in the past, you use the **passé composé**, and to describe conditions or tell about recurring events in the past, you use the **imparfait**. Like in English, adverbs can provide clues about which tense to use in French. Here are some words and expressions that can help you decide whether to use the **passé composé** or the **imparfait**.

PASSÉ COMPOSÉ	IMPARFAIT

un jour   lundi, mardi,
       mercredi...
    une fois
tout à coup   soudain
	toujours le lundi, le
	       mardi...
	    souvent
	de temps en d'habitude
	temps

C H A P I T R E 1 2

B. Underline the adverbs and adverbial expressions in the following sentences. Do these sentences describe a completed event or a regularly occurring event or condition in the past?

COMPLETED EVENT	REGULARLY OCCURRING EVENT OR CONDITION

1. J'allais souvent au cinéma.

2. De temps en temps, il faisait du camping.

3. Un jour, ma cousine est arrivée.

4. D'habitude, mon père était de bonne humeur.

5. Il pleuvait toujours au printemps.

6. D'abord, on a visité le musée de beaux arts.

7. Soudain, j'ai eu une idée.

C. Write original sentences to describe the past using a word or expression from each of the columns below. Be sure to use the tense that makes the most sense with each adverb.

d'habitude une fois un jour le dimanche soudain souvent d'abord de temps en temps	mon professeur je ils ma famille nous tu on mes amis	donner aller voir avoir être jouer visiter faire

1. _____

2. _____

3. _____

4. _____

5. _____

6. _____

7. _____

8. _____

D. What do the adverbs in the following sentences tell you about the events described?

1. Mon frère regardait souvent les dessins animés à la télé le samedi matin.

_____

_____

2. D'abord, on est allés au café. Ensuite, on a pris le métro pour aller voir la cathédrale.

_____

_____

CHAPITRE 12

Grammar of Allez, viens! French 3

CHAPITRE 1

■ THE PAST TENSE

In English You can talk about what happened in the past using the **past tense**, which consists of a single verb. Often these verb forms end in *-d* or *-ed*, but sometimes they are irregular.

Cindy **called**.
Billy **ran**.

You can also talk about the past using **the present perfect**. You may recall that present perfect includes a helping verb and a past form of the main verb. In an English present perfect, the helping verb is always a form of the verb *to have*.

Connie **has gone** to the store.
They **have carried** in the groceries.

A. Underline the complete verb in each sentence. Circle the helping verb if there is one.

1. Carl (has) written a letter to his congressman.

2. Fred married my sister.

3. Who let the cat in?

4. I have seen this movie before.

5. Cheryl hasn't received her invitation yet.

6. The newspaper arrived late again today.

In French You can talk about the past using the **passé composé**. The passé composé is made up of a helping verb and a past participle. The helping verb is usually a form of the verb **avoir**. Like English, French has some irregular past participles.

Michèle et Caroline **ont regardé** la télé.
<u>helping verb</u>   <u>past participle</u>

In some instances, the helping verb is a form of the verb **être**. Use the helping verb **être** instead of **avoir** with the following verbs:

aller	**arriver**	**descendre**	**entrer**	**monter**	**mourir**	**naître**
partir	**rentrer**	**rester**	**retourner**	**revenir**	**tomber**	**venir**

Christophe **est allé** à la banque.
<u>helping verb past participle</u>

You also use the helping verb **être** as the helping verb in the passé composé of reflexive verbs. Since the helping verb is **être**, the past participle matches the gender (masculine or feminine) and number (singular or plural) of the subject if the reflexive pronoun is the direct object of the action.

Elle s'**est levée** tôt ce matin.   BUT   Elle s'**est lavé** les cheveux.

B. Underline the verbs in the following sentences. Circle the helping verbs.

1. Francine s'*est* réveillée à six heures.

2. Paulette a mangé une pomme.

3. Tu as mis une cravate ce soir!

4. La pauvre Nanette est tombée d'un arbre.

5. Les Granger ont eu un accident de voiture.

6. J'ai fini tous mes devoirs avant huit heures.

7. Nous sommes restés chez Tante Huguette.

C. Complete the following sentences with the correct form of the helping verbs **avoir** or **être**.

1. Louise _____ **a** _____ perdu son passeport.

2. Mes cousins _____ pris le train pour aller à Nice.

3. Tu ne t' _____ pas lavé les cheveux?

4. Je _____ allée en Allemagne l'année dernière.

5. Est-ce qu'il _____ fait beau ce week-end?

6. Qui _____ commandé un sandwich au fromage?

7. Nous _____ lu le journal ce matin.

8. Quand est-ce que vous _____ arrivés?

D. Explain why, in the following sentences, one past participle agrees with the subject and the other doesn't, even though both use the helping verb **être**.

Annette s'est lavée.   Camille s'est cassé la jambe.

_____

_____

_____

_____

_____

CHAPITRE 2

■ PRONOUNS AND THEIR PLACEMENT

> **In English Direct Objects** are used to tell *whom* or *what,* and **indirect objects** are used to tell *for whom* or *to whom* an action is done.
>
> Mary gives Paul the flower.
> *What* does Mary give   the **flower**   (direct object)
> *To whom* does Mary give the flower?   to **Paul**   (indirect object)
>
> Direct and indirect objects can be replaced by the object pronouns: **me, you, him, her, it, us, you** *(plural),* and **them**.
>
> Mary gives Paul the **flower**. → Mary gives **it** to Paul.
> Mary gives the flower to **Paul**. → Mary gives **him** the flower.
>
> Notice that if the indirect object comes after the direct object, a preposition is used.

A. Underline the direct objects in the following sentences. Circle the indirect objects.

1. Frankie threw (me) the ball.

2. Lisa gave Phil a big party.

3. Caroline sent Bobby a package.

4. Our neighbor brought us our newspaper.

5. Lynn taught her son Spanish.

6. She sometimes buys herself roses.

> **In French Direct objects** are also used to tell *whom* or *what* and **indirect objects** are used to tell *to whom* or *for whom* an action is done.
>
> Marie donne la fleur à Paul.
> Qu'est-ce que Marie donne?   la **fleur**   (direct object)
> A qui Marie donne la fleur?   à **Paul**   (indirect object)
>
> • Direct objects are replaced by the pronouns: **me, te, nous, vous, le, la, l',** and **les**.
>
> • Indirect objects are replaced by the pronouns: **me, te, nous, vous, lui,** and **leur**.
>
> Marie donne la fleur à Paul. → Marie **la lui** donne.

subject   verb   indirect object   subject indirect object verb
Victor parle **à ses sœurs**.   Victor **leur** parle.

Besides direct and indirect object pronouns, you can also use **y, en,** and the reflexive pronoun **se**. The pronoun **y** can replace a phrase beginning with a preposition of location, such as **à** or **chez**. It often means *there*. The pronoun **en** replaces a phrase that begins with **de**.

As in English, you may want to use more than one pronoun in a sentence. The chart below shows the order in which to place pronouns in a single sentence.

me
te
se   →   le
nous   la   →   lui   →   y   →   en
vous   l'   leur
           les

B. Underline the direct objects in the following sentences. Draw two lines under any phrases that could be replaced by **y** or **en** and circle the indirect objects.

1. Marie-Laure est allée <u>à San Francisco</u>.

2. Achète cette robe!

3. Ils ont visité le musée.

4. Noémie voudrait trois tranches de jambon.

5. Florent va téléphoner à ses parents demain.

6. Tu donnes ton numéro de téléphone à Lola?

7. J'ai vu Daria au centre commercial.

C. Rewrite the sentences above using pronouns to replace the words you underlined and circled.

1. **Marie-Laure y est allée.** _____

2. _____

3. _____

4. _____

5. _____

6. _____

7. _____

D. Explain the use of the following pronoun and its placement.

Téléphone-moi!

_____

_____

_____

CHAPITRE 2

CHAPITRE 3

■ THE SUBJUNCTIVE

Pupil's Edition, Level 3, p. 69

In English Verbs may be in one of three moods. **indicative**, **imperative**, or **subjunctive**. Most verbs used in writing and speaking are in the **indicative** mood.

- The **indicative** mood is used to make statements of fact: She **sits** down.
- The **imperative** mood is used for commands: **Sit** down!

The **subjunctive** mood is not used frequently in English. The only common uses of the subjunctive mood are to express *necessity, importance, a condition contrary to fact,* and *a wish.*

> She acted as though I **were** her daughter. *(condition contrary to fact)*
> It is important that he **read** this book. *(importance)*
> I wish she **were** my sister. *(wish)*

A. For each of the following sentences, identify the mood of the verb in red type.

	INDICATIVE	IMPERATIVE	SUBJUNCTIVE
1. Please **hold** your applause until later.		✓	
2. La Paz **is** the world's highest capital city.			
3. If I **were** you, I wouldn't swim here.			
4. I think your sister **wants** to come with us.			
5. **Straighten** your room before you leave!			
6. Is it necessary that he **rehearse** now?			

In French As in English, verbs may also be in the **indicative**, **imperative**, or **subjunctive** mood.

- The **indicative** mood is used to make statements of fact. Nous **mangeons**.
- The **imperative** mood is used for commands. **Mange** ta soupe!

Unlike in English, the **subjunctive** mood is used frequently in French. Two of the most important uses of the subjunctive are to express obligation (often with **il faut que**) and to tell what you want (often with **vouloir que**).

> Il faut que Maxime **prenne** le métro. *(obligation)*
> Je veux que tu **fasses** tes devoirs. *(will)*

C H A P I T R E 3

B. For each of the following sentences, identify the mood of the verb in red.

	INDICATIVE	IMPERATIVE	SUBJUNCTIVE
	✓		

1. Je **peux** aller à la piscine cet aprèm?

2. Il faut que tu **sortes** le chien.

3. **Range** ta chambre!

4. Je voudrais qu'elle **vienne** tout de suite.

5. Au petit déjeuner, je **prends** des céréales.

In French The **present subjunctive** verb forms are based on the **ils/elles** forms of the **present indicative**. Drop the indicative ending and add **-e**, **-es**, **-e**, **-ions**, **-iez**, or **-ent**.

PRESENT INDICATIVE
Elles **sort~~ent~~**

PRESENT SUBJUNCTIVE

Il faut que je **sorte**　　　Il faut que nous **sortions**
Il faut que tu **sortes**　　　Il faut que vous **sortiez**
Il faut qu'il/elle **sorte**　　Il faut qu'ils/elles **sortent**

Certain verbs, such as **prendre** and **venir**, have different stems for the **nous** and **vous** forms.

Il faut qu'il **prenne** le bus.　BUT　Il faut que vous **preniez** le bus.
Tu veux que je **vienne** dimanche?　BUT　Tu veux que nous **venions** dimanche?

Other verbs have an irregular stem in all of their subjunctive forms. For example, the subjunctive stem for **faire** is **fass-**.

Le professeur veut que nous **fassions** nos devoirs.

Other verbs, such as **être**, have unique forms.

Il faut que tu **sois** polie, Marianne.

C. Compare the verb forms in the chart below. In your own words, explain how the subjunctive of the verb **prendre** is based on the indicative. What do you notice about the **ils/elles** forms?

PRESENT INDICATIVE		PRESENT SUBJUNCTIVE	
je prends	nous prenons	je <u>prenne</u>	nous <u>prenions</u>
tu prends	vous prenez	tu <u>prennes</u>	vous <u>preniez</u>
il/elle prend	ils/elles prennent	il/elle <u>prenne</u>	ils/elles <u>prennent</u>

_____

_____

_____

CHAPITRE 3

CHAPITRE 4

◼ THE INTERROGATIVE AND DEMONSTRATIVE PRONOUNS

> **In English** The **interrogative** phrases *which one* and *which ones* are used in questions to refer to something that has been previously mentioned. In the following sentence *which one* refers to <u>that car</u>.
>
> – I like <u>that car</u>. – **Which one**?
>
> The **demonstrative** phrases *this one, that one, these,* and *those* are used in statements to refer to something that has been previously mentioned.
>
> – Which car do you like? – **That one.**
>
> Notice how interrogative and demonstrative phrases can be used together.
>
> – I like <u>that car</u>. – **Which one?** – **That one**.

A. Underline the interrogative and demonstrative phrases in the following sentences. Then indicate what type each one is ?

	INTERROGATIVE	DEMONSTRATIVE
1.	✓	
2.		
3.		
4.		
5.		

1. <u>Which one</u> do you want?

2. Mary bought those.

3. You wanted her to bring which ones?

4. I really prefer this one.

5. These are his favorites.

> **In French** **Interrogative pronouns** are used to ask questions such as *which one(s)*. The forms of these pronouns agree in gender and number with the nouns they stand for.
>
> | | MASCULINE | FEMININE |
> |---|---|---|
> | SINGULAR | **lequel** | **laquelle** |
> | PLURAL | **lesquels** | **lesquelles** |
>
> **Demonstrative pronouns** are used to say *this one, that one, these,* or *those*. They also agree in gender and number with the nouns they stand for.
>
> | | SINGULAR | PLURAL |
> |---|---|---|
> | MASCULINE | **celui-là** | **ceux-là** |
> | FEMININE | **celle-là** | **celles-là** |
>
> Notice how interrogative and demonstrative pronouns can be used together once the referent has been made clear.
>
> | FEMININE | MASCULINE | MASCULINE PLURAL | FEMININE PLURAL |
> |---|---|---|---|
> | –J'aime cette montre. | –J'aime ce jean. | –J'aime ces pulls. | –J'aime ces roses. |
> | –**Laquelle**? | –**Lequel**? | –**Lesquels**? | –**Lequelles**? |
> | –**Celle-là**. | –**Celui-là**. | –**Ceux-là**. | –**Celles-là**. |

B. Underline the pronouns in the following sentences. Then incicate whether each one is interrogative or demonstrative?

	INTERROGATIVE	DEMONSTRATIVE
1		✓
2		
3		
4		
5		

1. Je prends celui-là.

2. Laquelle aimes-tu?

3. Lequel avez-vous vu?

4. Je déteste ceux-là.

5. Celles-là sont très chères.

C. Complete each response with either a demonstrative or an interrogative pronoun.

1. Pourquoi tu n'achètes pas ce disque compact?

   Parce que je préfère _____ **celui-là** _____.

2. Il aime cette montre.

   Moi, j'aime mieux _____.

3. Quel pantalon est-ce que tu veux?

   Je veux _____.

4. Elles sont jolies, ces cravates!

   Ah oui? _____?

5. Quelles lunettes vas-tu prendre?

   Je vais prendre _____.

6. Tu n'aimes pas ce pull?

   _____?

D. Respond to the following statement with an interrogative pronoun. Then, explain in your own words how you knew which form of the pronoun to use. What words told you its number or gender?

— Il est mignon, ce petit chat.

_____

_____

_____

_____

_____

CHAPITRE 5

> **In English** The **future tense** is used to talk about actions or events that are yet to take place. The future tense is formed by placing the word **will** before the base form of the verb.
>
> My grandchildren **will drive** electric cars.
> The people of the future **will** only **use** solar energy.
>
> To make a sentence in the future tense negative, you add *not* after *will. Will not* can combine to form the contraction *won't*.
>
> She **will not forget** what happened.
> She **won't forget** what happened.

A. In each of the following sentences, underline the helping verbs and circle the main verbs.

1. We will do the dishes after the movie.
2. Dad will be pleased with your grades.
3. I will not stay here past Saturday.
4. Martin won't hesitate to help us.
5. The couple will have a baby this fall.
6. Our team will win the game.

> **In French** As in English, the **future tense** is used to refer to events or actions that are yet to take place. The future tense is usually formed by adding the following endings to an infinitive: **-ai, -as, -a, -ons, -ez, -ont**.
>
> | | | |
> |---|---|---|
> | chercher → | je **chercherai** | nous **chercherons** |
> | | tu **chercheras** | vous **chercherez** |
> | | il/elle **cherchera** | ils/elles **chercheront** |
>
> In the case of **-re** verbs, drop the final **-e** before adding the future tense ending.
>
> apprendre → Bientôt, tu **apprendras** à nager.
>
> Some verbs are irregular in the future tense. Add the future ending to the following stems:
>
> | | | | |
> |---|---|---|---|
> | aller: **ir-** | devoir: **devr-** | faire: **fer-** | voir: **verr-** |
> | avoir: **aur-** | envoyer: **enverr-** | pouvoir: **pourr-** | venir: **viendr-** |
> | devenir: **deviendr-** | être: **ser-** | savoir: **saur-** | vouloir: **voudr-** |

B. In each of the following sentences, underline the stems of the verbs and circle the future endings.

1. Tes amis se marier(ont.)

2. Nous choisirons un métier.

3. Christine entrera à l'université.

4. Je voyagerai beaucoup.

5. Tu iras en Europe.

6. Lise deviendra médecin.

7. Vous verrez le monde.

C. The sentences below tell what's *going to happen* using **aller** and an infinitive. Rewrite them to tell what *will happen* using the future tense.

1. Je vais devenir ingénieur.

   Je deviendrai ingénieur.

2. Thomas va faire un long voyage.

   _____

3. Tu vas envoyer une lettre à une école technique.

   _____

4. Nous allons choisir une université.

   _____

5. Vous allez avoir des enfants.

   _____

6. Christelle et Olivier vont se marier.

   _____

7. Nous allons être très contents.

   _____

D. Fill in the left side of the chart with the forms of **avoir** in the present tense. Fill in the right side of the chart with the endings of the future tense. Then, compare the two charts. How might the similarities and differences help you remember how to talk about the future?

Avoir		Le Futur	
j' **ai** ___	nous _____	je choisirai **ai** ___	nous choisir_____
tu _____	vous _____	tu choisir_____	vous choisir_____
il _____	ils _____	il choisir_____	ils choisir _____

_____

_____

_____

CHAPITRE 5

In English The **conditional** is used to express *what would happen if* . . . as opposed to what usually happens. The conditional is formed by adding **would** to the base form of the verb.

> I **would drive** drive you home if I had a car.
> We **would** really **like** to go to the Bahamas.

A. In the following sentences underline the verbs that are in the conditional.

1. She <u>would help</u> you if you asked her to.

2. Joe would buy this bike if it were less expensive.

3. You would look handsome in that suit.

4. Would you like to go to the park?

5. I would love to meet your friends.

6. If they knew him better, they would believe his story.

7. He would never go on a safari.

8. What would you like to do after high school?

In French As in English, the **conditional** is used to express *what would happen if* . . . as opposed to what usually happens.

> Elle **viendrait** si elle avait le temps.
> Je **voudrais** aller au cinéma, mais j'ai des devoirs à faire.

The conditional is formed by combining the stems of the future tense with the imperfect endings **-ais**, **-ais**, **-ait**, **-ions**, **-iez**, **aient**. Remember, most future stems are the infinitive forms of the verb. As in the future tense, drop the final **-e** from **-re** verbs before adding the endings.

> Je **mangerais** bien une pizza ce soir.
> Il **vendrait** sa motocyclette si ses parents le lui permettaient.
> Nous **partirions** demain si nous pouvions.
> Marie **aurait** de meilleures notes si elle étudiait ses leçons.
> Ce **serait** chouette si elle venait passer ses vacances avec nous!

A sentence in the conditional often contains a **si** *(if)* clause. Notice that the **si** clause is in the **imparfait**.

imparfait   conditional
Si j'étais toi, je téléphonerais à tes parents.   *If I were you, I would call your parents.*

B. In the following sentences underline the verbs that are in the conditional mood. Circle any verbs in the imperfect.

1. S'il faisait beau, je jouerais au tennis.

2. Tu pourrais me passer du sel?

3. J'aimerais être avocate.

4. Ça serait super si tu pouvais venir cet été.

5. Mes cousins viendraient plus souvent si nous avions une grande maison.

6. Est-ce que vous voudriez visiter des châteaux?

7. Qu'est-ce que tu ferais à ma place?

C. Underline the verbs that correctly complete the following sentences.

1. Si je (tombais / tomberais) amoureux, je me (mariais / marierais).

2. Nous (cherchions / chercherions) un emploi, si nous (étions / serions) au chômage.

3. Si mes parents (gagnaient / gagneraient) plus d'argent, nous (voyagions / voyagerions).

4. S'ils (avaient / auraient) un enfant, ils (avaient / auraient) beaucoup de responsabilités.

5. J(e) (étais / serais) dans un groupe de rock, si je (jouais / jouerais) de la guitare.

6. Si elle (réussissait / réussirait) au bac, elle (allait / irait) à l'université.

7. Vous me (téléphoniez / téléphoneriez), si vous (vouliez / voudriez) me parler.

D. Rewrite the following sentence using the conditional mood. Then, explain how this change influences its meaning.

Je veux une glace.

_____

_____

_____

_____

_____

CHAPITRE 6

■ RECIPROCAL VERBS

In English When you use the expressions *one another* or *each other,* the action of the verb is **reciprocal**. As with reflexive verbs, the subject(s) receive(s) the action of the verb.

Sean and Lori like **each other.**

In English, if the meaning is clear enough, you don't have to say *each other.* In the sentence below, who will speak to whom is obvious, so you could leave out *to each other.*

Let's talk (**to each other**) on the phone tonight.

Because the reciprocity of action verbs takes place between several people or things, these verbs are necessarily plural.

A. Underline the reciprocal phrase (verb + pronoun) in each sentence.

1. Manuel and Robert help each other study for the test.

2. Elisa and Anne argue with each other all the time.

3. Now the girls aren't speaking to one another.

4. They finally made up with each other.

5. We like each other.

6. The family members support one another.

7. Ricardo and Lucy never lie to each other.

8. The students tell one another about their vacation.

In French **Reciprocal verbs** use some of the same pronouns as reflexive verbs: **se, nous,** and **vous**. These pronouns are plural and generally mean *each other.*

Nous **nous voyons** le week-end.　　*We **see each other** on weekends.*

In the **passé composé**, reciprocal verbs take the helping verb **être.**

When a verb takes a direct object, the past participle agrees with the pronoun.

Elles **se sont vues** à la gare.

When a verb takes an indirect object, the past participle does not agree with the pronoun.

Nous **nous sommes téléphoné.**

Besides **téléphoner,** other verbs that take indirect objects are **parler, dire, commander, offrir, demander,** and **conseiller.** Whenever you learn a verb, notice whether it takes a direct or an indirect object.

CHAPITRE 6

B. Underline the reciprocal pronoun in each sentence.

1. Nous <u>nous</u> aimons bien.

2. Vous vous disputez trop souvent.

3. Vous vous êtes rencontrés où?

4. Ils se sont offert des cadeaux.

5. Nous nous parlions rarement au lycée.

6. Ils se sont regardés et tout de suite, ils se sont plus.

7. Nous ne nous voyons jamais pendant le week-end.

8. Pourquoi Fatima et Alice se sont disputées?

C. Rewrite the following sentences in the **passé composé**. Remember to make the past participles agree with their direct objects.

1. Nous nous voyons dimanche.

   Nous nous sommes vu(e)s dimanche.

2. Julie et Jean se retrouvent à la piscine.

   _____

3. Carole et Charlotte se réconcilient.

   _____

4. Est-ce que Georges et toi, vous vous aimez beaucoup?

   _____

5. Nous nous disons la vérité.

   _____

6. Elles se parlent aussi souvent que possible.

   _____

D. Do the sentences below take a direct or an indirect object? How can you tell?

1. J'ai vu le film.

   _____

   _____

   _____

2. Il a téléphoné à Pam.

   _____

   _____

   _____

CHAPITRE 7

◼ USING THE SUBJUNCTIVE

In English You learned earlier that the **subjunctive** mood is used to express *necessity, importance, a condition contrary to fact, or a wish.*

IMPORTANCE	It is important that you **be** on time.
CONDITION CONTRARY TO FACT	If I **were** in his shoes, I would apologize.
WISH	Lauren wishes she **were** taller.

A. In the following sentences, are the verbs in red in the indicative or subjunctive mood?

	INDICATIVE	SUBJUNCTIVE
1. I recommend that he **arrive** early.		✓
2. It is clear that she **is** mistaken.		
3. If only the story **were** true!		
4. If I **were** you, I'd write a book.		
5. I think that he **has** a girlfriend.		
6. They demanded that the man **give** them his name.		

In French The **subjunctive** is used more frequently than it is in English. In earlier chapters, you learned to use the subjunctive with the expressions **il faut que** and **vouloir que**.

> **Je veux que** tu *viennes* avec moi.
> **Il faut que** tu *sois* à l'heure.

Like English, certain expressions of *necessity* also call for the subjunctive.

Il est necessaire que...	*It is necessary that...*
Il est essentiel que...	*It is essential that...*
Il faudrait que...	*It would be necessary to...*
Il vaudrait mieux que...	*It would be better to...*

Additionally, certain expressions of *possibility* or *doubt* automatically call for the subjunctive.

Il est possible que...	*It is possible that...*
Il se peut que...	*It could be that...*
Je ne crois pas que...	*I don't believe that...*
Je ne pense pas que...	*I don't think that....*
Ça m'étonnerait que...	*That would surprise me if...*
Je ne suis pas sûr(e) que...	*I'm not sure that...*
Je ne suis pas certain(e) que...	*I'm not certain that...*

Certain phrases that express *emotions* are also used with the subjunctive.

Je suis désolé(e) que...	*I'm sorry that...*
Je suis heureux/heureuse que...	*I'm happy that...*
J'ai peur que...	*I'm afraid that...*

While the subjunctive is always preceded by **que**, not all expressions with **que** call for the subjunctive. Try to learn by heart each expression that takes the subjunctive.

B. In the following sentences, are the verbs in red in the indicative or subjunctive mood?

	INDICATIVE	SUBJUNCTIVE
1.	✓	
2.		
3.		
4.		
5.		
6.		

1. Je sais que tu n'**aimes** pas les épinards.

2. Il est possible qu'il **revienne** demain.

3. J'ai peur qu'elle ne **réussisse** pas

4. Je suis certain que tu **es** un enfant sage.

5. Voici le livre que je **veux**.

6. Il est important que vous **fassiez** le ménage.

C. Complete the following sentences, using the subjunctive when necessary.

1. Je suis certain que (qu') __il viendra ce soir._____

2. Il faudrait que (qu') _____

3. Il n'est pas sûr que (qu') _____

4. Il se peut que (qu') _____

5. Nous savons que (qu') _____

6. Il est essentiel que (qu') _____

7. Je suis désolé que (qu') _____

D. Explain the use of different moods in the following sentences. Tell why one uses the subjunctive and the other does not.

Je pense qu'il **est** gentil. Je ne pense pas qu'il **soit** méchant.

_____

_____

_____

_____

_____

CHAPITRE 8

■ THE COMPARATIVE

In English To make **comparisons** with nouns, you can use **more. . . than**, **fewer. . . than**, **less. . . than**, **as much. . . as**, or **as many. . . as**, along with the noun.

There are **fewer** boxes here **than** there.   T.J. has **as many** games **as** Mark.

To make comparisons with verbs, you use **more than**, **less than**, and **as much as**.

Mary works **less than** George.

To make comparisons with adjectives and adverbs, you use **more... than**, **less. . . than**, and **as. . . as**.

My book is **more** interesting **than** yours.   Timmy runs **less** fast **than** Jeremy.

When the adjective has only one or two syllables, instead of using *more,* you add the suffix **-er** at the end of the adjective.

Frances is **taller than** Jim.

The comparative forms of the adjective *good* and the adverb *well* are both **better**. The comparitive forms of the adjective *bad* and the adverb *badly* are **worse**.

This painting is **better than** that one.   Phil plays tennis **better than** me.

A. Underline the comparative phrases in the following sentences. Are the items carrying the comparison nouns, adjectives, adverbs, or verbs?

	Nouns	Adjectives	Adverbs	Verbs
1.		✓		
2.				
3.				
4.				
5.				

1. My suitcase is <u>heavier than</u> yours.

2. This poster is more colorful than that one.

3. John ate more pizza than Rachid.

4. Luis speaks more softly than Rachel.

5. They study more than Ellen.

In French To make comparisons with nouns, use **plus de... que**, **moins de... que** or **autant de... que**.

Il a **plus de** C.D. **que** Stéphanie.   J'ai **autant d'**argent **que** toi.

To make comparisons with adjectives and adverbs, use **plus... que**, **moins... que**, or **aussi... que**.

Julie est **moins** courageuse **que** Chloé.   Elise conduit **moins** vite **que** Sabine.

The adjective *bon* has special comparative forms:

bon →	**meilleur**	bons →	**meilleurs**
bonne →	**meilleure**	bonnes→	**meilleures**

To make comparisons with verbs, use **plus que**, **moins que**, or **autant que** just after the verb.

Léa mange **plus que** Paul.   Elle parle **autant que** Line.

B. Underline the comparative phrases in the following sentences. Are the items carrying the comparison nouns, adjectives, adverbs, or verbs?

	NOUNS	ADJECTIVES	ADVERBS	VERBS
1.				✓
2.				
3.				
4.				
5.				
6.				
7.				

1. Je <u>chante</u> mieux <u>que</u> Sylvie.

2. Les gens sont plus pressés à Paris qu'à Reno.

3. Il y a plus d'animaux dans la forêt qu'en ville.

4. L'histoire, c'est plus intéressant que les maths.

5. Les cafés sont meilleurs à New York qu'à Dakar.

6. Laure nage moins bien que Philippe.

7. J'ai autant de livres que Michèle.

C. Unscramble the following words to form comparative sentences.

1. s'habille / bien / Cécile / Yvette / moins / qu'

   Cécile s'habille moins bien qu'Yvette.

2. Louise / petite / plus / Marc / est / que

   _____

3. mieux / chantent / moi / que / elles

   _____

4. Lise / autant / d' / qu' / a / Elisabeth / argent

   _____

5. Stéphane / aussi / que / drôle / êtes / vous

   _____

6. meilleures / quiches / les / sont / soupe / la / que

   _____

D. In your own words, explain why there are several forms of **meilleur**, but only one form of **mieux**.

   _____
   _____
   _____
   _____

French 3 Allez, viens!, Chapter 8

CHAPITRE 9

■ NEGATIVE EXPRESSIONS

In English Most **negative expressions** contain the word *not*.

He is **not** going.   He is **not** going **yet**.   He is **not** going **anymore**.

Sometimes there is more than one way to express a negative concept in English.

He is **not** going **anywhere**.   He is going **nowhere**.
I do **not** see **anybody**.   I see **no one**.   I see **nobody**.

Nobody, no one, and **nothing** can be the subject of a sentence.

Nobody came to the party.   **Nothing** happened.

The elements of the expression **neither... nor** immediately precede the words they modify.

I like **neither** pretzels **nor** potato chips.   **Neither** Bob **nor** Ted called yesterday.

A. Underline the negative expressions in the following sentences.

1. Don does <u>not</u> go <u>anywhere</u> during the week.

2. Nobody brought anything to drink.

3. I like neither spiders nor snakes.

4. Nothing exciting ever happens here.

5. Tina has nothing to give him for his birthday.

In French Like **ne... pas**, other **negative expressions** have at least two parts: **ne** (or **n'**) and another word or expression.

ne... pas encore	*not yet*
ne... jamais	*never*
ne... plus	*not anymore*
ne... personne	*no one / not anyone*
ne... rien	*nothing*
ne... ni... ni	*neither... nor*
ne... aucun	*no / not any*
ne... nulle part	*nowhere*

As in English, most negative expressions function as adverbs. Both **personne ne...** and **rien ne...** can function as subjects of a sentence.

In the expression **ne... ni... ni...**, **ne** is placed immediately before the verb and **ni... ni...** immediately before the words they modify.

Je **ne** connais **ni** Julie **ni** Laura.   Il **n'**aime **ni** la pizza **ni** la quiche.

B. Underline the negative expressions in the following sentences.

1. Je _ne_ fais _rien_ cet après-midi

2. Elle n'est allée nulle part pendant les vacances.

3. Personne ne sait jouer aux cartes?

4. Délia n'est pas encore arrivée?

5. Rien ne passe à la télé ce soir.

6. Je n'aime ni la chimie ni la biologie.

7. Vous n'avez aucun livre de Saint-Exupéry?

C. Unscramble the following sentences that contain negative expressions.

1. fais / jamais / vaisselle / tu / la / ne

   Tu ne fais jamais la vaisselle.

2. ni / Karine / n' / a / son / manteau / casquette / sa / ni

   _____

3. leurs / encore / devoirs / fini / ont / pas / ils / n'

   _____

4. ne / aller / je / nulle part / veux /

   _____

5. la / est / dernière / arrivé / n' / rien / semaine /

   _____

6. y / au / personne / avait / n' / supermarché / il

   _____

D. Explain the difference in the placement of **ne... personne** in the following sentences.

Personne n'est venu. Il ne voit personne.

_____

_____

_____

_____

_____

In English **Relative pronouns** are used to join related statements in a single sentence.

> I like the photo. + You took the photo. → I like the photo **that** you took.

Relative pronouns can function as subjects, direct objects, and objects of prepositions within a subordinate clause.

SUBJECT	I like the boy **who** talked to me yesterday.
OBJECT	I liked the movie **that** I saw yesterday. Here is the girl **whom** I invited. This poster, **which** I bough yesterday, is for my sister.
OBJECT OF PREPOSITION	The man with **whom** I spoke is from Nice. The book of **which** I spoke is here.

Whose is the posessive form of *who.*

> The people **whose** car is in the driveway are friends of my parents.

Notice that in English, you can sometimes leave out the relative pronoun.

> The dog ate the pie [that] you baked.

A. Underline the relative pronouns in the following sentences. If the pronoun is omitted, place an arrow where it would appear. Are the pronouns subjects or objects? Do they stand for people or things?

	SUBJECT	OBJECT	PEOPLE	THINGS
1. Mandy broke the statue that she bought.		✓		✓
2. This is the student for whom I voted.				
3. I like the flowers she brought me.				
4. Jolene is the one who called this morning.				
5. I know the boy whom you saw.				

1. Mandy broke the statue <u>that</u> she bought.

2. This is the student for whom I voted.

3. I like the flowers she brought me.

4. Jolene is the one who called this morning.

5. I know the boy whom you saw.

In French **Relative pronouns** serve the same purpose as they do in English. They join related statements in a single sentence. As in English, they can be subjects, direct objects, or objects of prepositions. They can refer to people or things.

Use **qui** as the subject of a clause, whether it is a person or a thing.

> Il s'agit d'une femme **qui** a perdu la mémoire.
> C'est le seul film **qui** commence avant huit heures.

Use **que** as the object of a clause, whether it is a person or a thing.

> Sabrina a invité une fille **que** j'aime beaucoup. Sandrine aime bien le livre **qu'**elle a lu.

Drop the **-e** off of **que** before a vowel sound, but do not drop the **-i** from **qui.**

Use the relative pronoun **dont** when the noun you're replacing is the object of a preposition such as **de.** Notice how **dont** is used to combine the following sentences.

> Tu connais l'actrice. + Il parle **de** l'actrice. → Tu connais l'actrice **dont** il parle.
> *You know the actress. He's speaking about the actress.* →
> *You know the actress **about whom** he's speaking.*

Dont can mean *whose, about whom, for whom, about which, for which,* or *of which.*

CHAPITRE 9

B. Underline the relative pronouns in the following sentences. Are they subjects or objects? Do they stand for people or things?

	Subjects	Objects	People	Things
1.	✓			✓
2.				
3.				
4.				
5.				
6.				
7.				

1. C'est un film <u>qui</u> fait rire.

2. Nadia est une fille que je connais bien.

3. La Guadeloupe est une île dont on rêve.

4. Luc a raconté une histoire que je ne crois pas.

5. J'aime bien le cadeau qu'elle m'a donné.

6. Il est où, le restaurant dont elle t'a parlé?

7. Je me souviens d'un acteur qui est très drôle.

C. Combine the sentences below using relative pronouns.

1. Le professeur est sympa. + Tu m'as parlé du professeur. →

   Le professeur dont tu m'as parlé est sympa.

2. Où sont les boissons? + Maman a acheté les boissons. →

   _____

3. J'aime bien l'hôtel. + La concierge a recommandé un hôtel. →

   _____

4. J'ai connu la fille. + La fille habite à côté de chez nous. →

   _____

5. C'est la voiture. + La voiture a causé un accident. →

   _____

D. Explain how you can tell the difference between a subject and an object. Use the following sentences as examples.

   C'est le médecin que je préfère.   C'est le médecin qui a sauvé ma vie.

   _____

   _____

   _____

   _____

   _____

CHAPITRE 10

■ THE SUPERLATIVE

> **In English** **Superlatives** are used to single out something as *the most* or *the least*.
> - To form the superlative of superiority of most adjectives and adverbs that have one or two syllables, you use the definite article **the** before the adjective or adverb and the suffix **−(e)st** at the end of the adjective or adverb. For other adjectives and adverbs, you use **the most** before the adjective or adverb.
>
> ADJECTIVES | ADVERBS
>
> That's **the great**est story I ever heard.   Jonathan runs **the fastest** in his class.
> This is **the most** entertaining show!   He's the one who comes here **the most** regularly.
>
> The superlative of *good* and *well* is **the best**; the superlative of *bad* is **the worst**.
>
> - Superlatives can also modify nouns and verbs.
>
> She is the one with **the most** friends. (noun superlative)
> My brother is the one who watches sports **the most**. (verb superlative)
>
> To form the superlative of inferiority, you add **the least** before adjectives, adverbs, and uncountable nouns, and after verbs. With countable nouns, you use **the fewest**.

A. Underline the superlative phrases in the following sentences. Is the item modified by each superlative an adjective, an adverb, a noun, or a verb?

	ADJECTIVES	ADVERBS	NOUNS	VERBS
1. Frieda is the kindest person I know.	✓			
2. It is Paul who writes me the most regularly.				
3. Of all my friends, Jack talks the most.				
4. Barbara has the least time among all of us.				

> **In French** **Superlatives** serve the same purpose as in English. They are usually formed using a definite article and **plus** or **moins**.
> - As in English, superlatives can modify adjectives. In that case the definite articles **le/l'**, **la**, or **les** are part of the superlative phrase. Both articles and adjectives agree in gender and number with the noun. If an adjective usually precedes the noun, form the superlative as follows.
>
> Thomas est **le plus** grand.   Mélanie est **la plus** grande.
>
> If an adjective usually follows the noun, use two definite articles, one before the noun and another before **plus** or **moins**.
>
> C'est **la fille la plus** intelligente de la classe.
>
> The superlative of the adjective **bon** is **le meilleur**; the superlative of **bonne** is **la meilleure**.
>
> C'est **le meilleur** fromage de la région.   Emilie es **la meilleure** éleve.

> • Superlatives can also modify nouns, adverbs, and verbs. In that case, the masculine article **le** always precedes **plus** and **moins**.
>
> C'est moi qui ai **le plus** d'amis. (noun superlative)
> C'est Julien qui court **le plus** vite. (adverb superlative)
> C'est Lucien qui travaille **le moins**. (verb superlative)
>
> The superlative of the adverb **bien** is **le mieux**.

B. Underline the superlative phrases in the following sentences. Are the items modified by the superlative adjectives, adverbs, nouns, or verbs?

	ADJECTIVES	ADVERBS	NOUNS	VERBS
1. C'est François qui court le moins vite.		✓		
2. Kevin et Michel sont mes meilleurs amis.				
3. Amélie est la fille la plus sage de notre famille.				
4. C'est Romain qui m'amuse le plus.				
5. C'est dans cette ville qu'il y a le moins de pollution.				
6. Dorothée est l'élève qui travaille le mieux.				
7. Les Salines est la plus belle plage du monde.				

C. Rewrite the following sentences, changing the adverbs or adjectives into superlatives.

1. Toi, tu chantes bien.

   Toi, tu chantes le mieux.

2. Maryse saute très haut.

   _____

3. Florence n'est pas gentille.

   _____

4. Viviane ne court pas vite.

   _____

5. Christophe et Janine sont sérieux.

   _____

6. Nous nous parlons souvent au téléphone.

   _____

In English When you say that you **had done** something before something else in the past, you're using the past perfect. The **past perfect** is made up of the past tense of *have*, **had**, and a past participle.

>She **had** already **arrived** when I got there.

Sometimes the previous action is implied rather than stated.

>I **had seen** the movie before.

A. In each of the sentences below, underline the verbs in the past perfect.

1. She <u>had</u> always <u>considered</u> Lois a close friend.

2. They had not forgotten us after all.

3. We had just started to eat when the phone rang.

4. A huge spider had spun a web outside the door.

5. Charlene had never been to a circus before.

6. We had drunk some water before starting the race.

In French To tell what happened in the past before something else, you use the **plus-que-parfait**.

>J'**avais allumé** la télé quand le téléphone a sonné.
>*I had turned on the TV when the phone rang.*

The **plus-que-parfait** is made up of the imperfect form of the helping verb, **avoir** or **être**, and the past participle of the main verb.

As in the **passé composé**, when the helping verb is **être**, the past participle usually agrees with the subject.

>Elle **était partie** quand le spectacle a commencé.

B. In each of the sentences below, underline the verbs that make up the **plus-que-parfait**.

1. Nous <u>avions déménagé</u> l'année d'avant.

2. Ils étaient allés en France.

3. J'avais oublié son adresse.

4. Marithé avait téléphoné à Pierre.

5. Christelle s'était fait mal au pied en marchant.

6. Micheline avait vite fait le ménage.

C. First, decide what helping verb is needed to form the **plus-que-parfait** in each of the statements below. Then complete the sentences with the correct form of the helping verbs.

	AVOIR	ETRE
		✓

1. Géraldine ___**était**___ allée au café avant la piscine.

2. Tu n'_____ pas passé ton bac avant ton séjour en Angleterre?

3. Les Martin _____ déjà acheté leur maison quand Li est arrivée à Chartres.

4. Pauline et Xavier s' _____ rencontrés bien avant 1995.

5. Tu savais que Félix s' _____ cassé le bras, toi?

6. Avant d'écrire son devoir, il _____ fait beaucoup de recherche.

D. For each of the sentences below, put the verb in parentheses in the **plus-que-parfait**. Don't forget agreements of past participles when necessary.

1. Tu savais qu'il _____**était parti**_____ (partir) au Canada?

2. On m'a dit que Brigitte et Jean _____ (se marier).

3. Je ne savais pas que tu _____ (avoir) un accident.

4. Vous saviez que Didier _____ (acheter) une moto?

5. Nous _____ (prendre) des photos, puis on a perdu l'appareil-photo.

6. Maman m'a demandé si j'_____ (faire) la vaisselle.

E. Compare the meanings of the two sentences below. Then, in your own words, explain how the two tenses are formed differently.

Vous êtes sortis.   Vous étiez sortis.

_____

_____

_____

_____

_____

_____

> **In English** The **relative pronoun** *what* can be used to link a main clause and a subordinate clause.
>
> Sometimes *what* replaces un unnamed antecedent.
>
> > I don't know **what** I can do about it.   Tell me **what** happened.
>
> Sometimes *what* stands for *something that.*
>
> > **What** *(Something that)* I really like is bread pudding.
> > Bread pudding is **what** *(something that)* I really like.
>
> **What** can be either the subject or the object of a clause.
>
> > I know **what** happened. (subject)
> > I know **what** Max got you for your birthday. (object)

A. Underline the relative pronouns in the following sentences. Are they subjects or objects?

SUBJECTS	OBJECT
	✓

1. I don't know <u>what</u> you're talking about.

2. They liked what they saw in Rome.

3. What's interesting is the color of this house.

4. They don't know what's best for them.

5. I'll tell you what she likes.

6. No one knows what will happen next.

> **In French** The **relative pronouns** *ce qui* and *ce que* both mean *what.*
>
> - **Ce qui** is the subject of the clause it introduces. It is usually followed by a verb.
>
>   > **Ce qui** est chouette, c'est le carnaval à La Nouvelle-Orléans.
>   > Je ne sais pas **ce qui** est arrivé à Denis.
>
> - **Ce que** (or **ce qu'**) is the object of the clause it introduces. It is usually followed by a subject.
>
>   > **Ce que** j'aime surtout ici, c'est les beignets.
>   > Fais **ce que** tu peux.
>
> Note that, just like *what,* both **ce qui** and **ce que** can be in the middle of a sentence, when they connect two clauses together.

B. Underline the relative pronouns in the following sentences. Are the pronouns subjects or objects?

	SUBJECTS	OBJECT
		✓

1. <u>Ce que</u> je mange, c'est du jambalaya.

2. Je ne sais pas ce qu'on met dans le gombo.

3. Ce qui m'intéresse surtout comme musique, c'est le jazz.

4. Ce qu'on va manger ce soir est super!

5. Dis-moi vite ce qui est arrivé!

6. Ils m'ont servi ce que je voulais.

C. Complete the following statements with the correct relative pronoun. Don't forget that **ce que** becomes **ce qu'** before a vowel sound.

1. Tu ne nous a pas dit _____**ce que**_____ tu as vu en Louisiane.

2. _____ me plaît ici, c'est les grands arbres et les maisons de style colonial.

3. Tu sais _____ est arrivé à Julien? Il a perdu son portefeuille!

4. _____ elle n'aime pas du tout, c'est les plats épicés.

5. Je ne sais pas _____ je vais prendre. Tout a l'air si bon!

6. _____ prend beaucoup de temps, c'est de préparer un gombo.

D. Explain the use of the relative pronouns in the following sentences. Tell why one sentence uses **ce qui** and the other **ce que.**

Ce qui me passionne, c'est les livres de science-fiction.   Je ne sais pas ce que je vais mettre ce soir.

_____

_____

_____

_____

_____

CHAPITRE 12

■ USING THE FUTURE

Pupil's Edition, Level 3, p. 348

> **In English** You use the present tense to talk about future events after **when** or **as soon as**.
>
> As soon as the train **arrives** (present), we **will find** (future) our seats.
>
> When Billy **is** (present) twenty-five, he **will have** (future) a good job.
>
> Remember, the future is formed by *will* plus the base form of the main verb.

A. In each of the following sentences, underline any verbs that are in the future tense.

1. When I finish high school, I <u>will travel</u>.

2. As soon as the guests leave, we will get some sleep.

3. When Martin arrives, we will celebrate.

4. The ship will depart as soon as everyone is on board.

5. Candace will return to work when she recovers from the accident.

6. Mrs. Sanders will retire as soon as the company finds a replacement.

> **In French** Unlike English, when you talk about events that will happen in the future, using **quand** (*when*) or **dès que** (*as soon as*), both clauses are in the future tense.
>
> Dès qu'elle **arrivera**, nous lui **parlerons**.
> Quand j'**irai** en Afrique, je **prendrai** beaucoup de photos.

B. In each of the following sentences, underline the verbs that are in the future tense.

1. Quand tu <u>iras</u> aux Jeux olympiques, tu <u>seras</u> content.

2. Je serai heureuse dès que j'arriverai.

3. Quand on rentrera à la maison, je me coucherai.

4. Dès que tu trouveras le temps, tu viendras nous voir.

5. Sophie cherchera un emploi quand elle aura son diplôme.

6. Dès que les cours seront finis, nous partirons en vacances.

7. Quand il neigera, on construira un bonhomme de neige.

C H A P I T R E 1 2

French 3 Allez, viens!, Chapter 12 — Grammar Tutor **117**

Copyright © by Holt, Rinehart and Winston. All rights reserved.

C. Complete the following statements and questions by conjugating the verbs in parentheses in the future tense.

1. Quand tu _____**seras**_____ (être) en France, tu _____**verras**_____ (voir) beaucoup de petites voitures.

2. Je vous _____ (écrire) dès que j' _____ (arriver) là-bas.

3. Nous _____ (aller) au café quand nous _____ (avoir) le temps.

4. Dès que Josique _____ (apprendre) la nouvelle, elle nous _____ (téléphoner).

5. Quand ils _____ (savoir) que je suis ici, ils _____ (venir) me voir.

6. Qu'est-ce que vous _____ (faire) quand vous _____ (avoir) 25 ans?

D. Complete the sentences below with a logical ending in the future tense.

1. Quand je serai en vacances, _**je partirai en France.**_____

2. Quand j'aurai dix-huit ans, _____

3. Dès que j'aurai mon diplôme, _____

4. Quand j'aurai assez d'argent, _____

5. Quand j'aurai trente ans, _____

6. Dès que j'aurai une nouvelle voiture, _____

7. Quand j'aurai des enfants, _____

8. Quand j'aurai le temps, _____

E. Consider why French speakers put clauses after **quand** and **dès que** in the future tense. Does this make sense to you? Why or why not?

_____

_____

_____

_____

_____

CHAPITRE 12

Answers

Allez, viens! French 1

Answers

Answers

CHAPITRE 1

■ NEGATIVE STATEMENTS

A. 1. My sister is <u>not</u> going home until later. (negative)
2. They are from San Francisco. (affirmative)
3. I <u>can't</u> see well without my glasses. (negative)
4. She <u>doesn't</u> like to play with dolls. (negative)
5. I'm studying French and English. (affirmative)
6. Our car <u>wouldn't</u> start this morning. (negative)

B. 1. J'ai quatorze ans. (affirmative)
2. Elle <u>n'</u>aime <u>pas</u> les escargots. (negative)
3. Thuy et Isabelle adorent le cinéma. (affirmative)
4. Tu <u>n'as pas</u> douze ans. (negative)
5. Nous <u>n'</u>aimons <u>pas</u> regarder la télévision. (negative)
6. Eric aime bien voyager. (affirmative)

C. 1. Je n'aime pas les examens.
2. Tu ne préfères pas la pizza.
3. Sandrine n'aime pas danser.
4. François n'adore pas le sport.
5. Tu n'as pas onze ans.
6. Vous n'aimez pas nager.
7. Nous n'adorons pas la salade.

D. Answers will vary. Possible answers:
Similarities: In both languages, you add a negative word or words next to the verb. You may sometimes form a contraction when making a statement negative. Differences: In French, two words, **ne** and **pas,** are placed around the verb to make a sentence negative, but in English you just add the word *not*. In English, contractions are not required. In French, **ne** must change to **n'** before a vowel or vowel sound.

■ DEFINITE ARTICLES

A. 1. They bought (the) house next door. (singular, no gender)
2. She made a chocolate cake for (the) boys. (plural, masculine)
3. (The) businessman is wearing a funny tie. (singular, masculine)
4. She put (the) new <u>tools</u> away. (plural, no gender)
5. (The) ship sailed to Martinique. (singular, no gender)
6. John painted (the) houses in one day. (plural, no gender)
7. (The) girls love (the) cat. (plural, feminine; singular, no gender)

B. 1. Sophie adore (la) glace. (singular, feminine)
2. Ils aiment bien (le) magasin. (singular, masculine)
3. Tu n'aimes pas (les) hamburgers? (plural, masculine)
4. Je préfère (les) frites. (plural, feminine)
5. Vous aimez (l') anglais? (singular, masculine)

C. 1. le
2. les
3. la
4. l'
5. les
6. le
7. les
8. le, l'

D. Answers will vary. Possible answer:
Item number 3 is different from the others because it refers to a specific noun, the beach, whereas the other items refer to general categories or concepts.

■ SUBJECT PRONOUNS

A. 1. (She) plays tennis every day.
2. <u>The pilot</u> landed the plane with ease.
3. <u>The movers</u> are carrying a grand piano.
4. (You) look great today!
5. <u>Marie</u> is seldom late.
6. (We) like pizza.
7. (They)'re very happy.

B. 1. (Vous) aimez le français?
2. <u>Lisette</u> adore le sport.
3. <u>Monsieur et Madame Hupert</u> aiment le cinéma.
4. (J')ai quatorze ans.
5. (Nous) aimons les escargots.
6. <u>M. Roland</u> n'aime pas faire du sport.
7. (Elle) adore le chocolat.

Answers

C. 1. elle; Nicole should be underlined.
2. il; Philippe should be underlined.
3. nous; Michèle and moi should be underlined.
4. il; Jean should be underlined.
5. elle; Danielle should be underlined.
6. ils; M. and Mme Roland should be underlined
7. elles; Claudette and Marie-Claire should be underlined
8. ils; Bruno and Robert should be underlined

D. Answers will vary. Possible answers:
1. M. et Mme Roland: Ils is the subject pronoun that stands for a mixed group of males and females.
2. Claudette et Marie-Claire: Elles is the pronoun that stands for two or more females.
3. Bruno et Robert: Ils is the subject pronoun that stands for two or more males.

■ SUBJECT-VERB AGREEMENT

A. 1. We ride our bikes to school sometimes.
2. Gary rides his bike to school, too.
3. Jeannette and Sandra like football.
4. Sandra likes school, too.
5. You and Peter go to the movies on Fridays.
6. I play sports after school.

B. 1. Tu aimes bien l'école?
2. Micheline adore les maths.
3. Les amis parlent au téléphone.
4. J'étudie les maths.
5. Nous adorons les vacances.
6. M. et Mme Blanchard, vous regardez la télé?

C. 1. nage
2. regardent
3. écoutes
4. dansons
5. étudiez
6. voyage
7. aimes
8. regardent
9. parle

D. Answers will vary. Possible answer:
If you learn one **-er** verb, you can follow its pattern when using other **-er** verbs.
Example: Elle parle français.

CHAPITRE 2

■ CONTRADICTING A NEGATIVE STATEMENT

A. 1. affirm
2. contradict
3. contradict
4. affirm
5. contradict
6. contradict

B. 1. oui
2. si
3. oui
4. si
5. oui
6. si

C. 1. Oui, j'aime le sport. OR Oui, nous aimons le sport.
2. Si, Mélanie (elle) aime les sciences.
3. Si, j'ai chimie ce matin.
4. Oui, Thuy (elle) adore l'anglais.
5. Si, Michel et Suzanne (ils) ont espagnol.
6. Si, elle aime bien voyager.

D. Answers will vary. Possible answer:
—Elle a chorale le mardi?
—Oui, elle a chorale le mardi et le jeudi.
—Elle n'aime pas la musique?
—Si, elle aime bien la musique.

E. In English, you contradict an affirmative statement with "no" and a negative statement with "yes." You also use the pitch of your voice and add stress to important words. In French, you contradict a negative statement by using the word **si** instead of the word **oui.** They are different because English doesn't have a single word like **si** to use for the purpose of contradicting.

■ IRREGULAR VERBS

A. 1. We play in the school band. (regular)
2. She is a good girl. (irregular)
3. I have a black and white rabbit. (irregular)
4. You go to the store on Tuesdays. (irregular)
5. Her father always bakes cookies. (regular)
6. They rest after the game. (regular)
7. Sandy loves pizza. (regular)
8. They are very tired. (irregular)

Answers

B. 1. J'adore le sport. (regular)
2. Tu _as_ quels cours aujourd'hui? (irregular)
3. Vous _parlez_ au téléphone. (regular)
4. Nous _aimons_ surtout le chocolat. (regular)
5. Ils _regardent_ la télévision. (regular)
6. Elle _a_ chimie maintenant. (irregular)
7. Lucie _étudie_ le français. (regular)
8. Eugène et Carole _ont_ allemand. (irregular)

C. 1. as
2. aime
3. a
4. adorons
5. avez
6. ai
7. aimons

D. Answers will vary. Possible answer:
Regular **-er** verbs have the same pattern of endings: **-e, -es, -e, -ons, -ez, -ent.** The forms of **avoir** are completely different from these and do not follow a pattern.

CHAPITRE 3

■ INDEFINITE ARTICLES

A. 1. I brought in _the_ plants last night. (definite)
2. Lucy is carrying _a_ heavy suitcase. (indefinite)
3. You don't have _the_ herbal shampoo? (definite)
4. _The_ test wasn't very hard. (definite)
5. _An_ ant just crawled onto my foot. (indefinite)
6. Did you mail _a_ card to Aunt Ruthie? (indefinite)
7. Did you give _the_ book to John? (definite)

B. 1. Vous avez _un_ crayon rouge? (masculine, singular)
2. C'est _une_ règle? (feminine, singular)
3. Elle a _un_ sac noir. (masculine, singular)
4. Nous avons _des_ feuilles de papier. (feminine, plural)
5. Jing-Yu a _un_ ordinateur. (masculine, singular)
6. Tu as _une_ gomme? (feminine, singular)
7. Il a _une_ cassette? (feminine, singular)
8. Nous n'avons pas _de_ livres. (masculine, plural)

C. 1. d'
2. un
3. des
4. de
5. une
6. des
7. de
8. des

D. Answers will vary. Possible answer:
Tu as la radio?
Tu as une radio?
La radio refers to a specific radio. Both parties in the conversation know what particular radio the speaker is talking about. **Une radio** refers to a radio in general (any radio), rather than a specific one.

■ DEMONSTRATIVE ADJECTIVES

A. 1. _This_ homework is not mine. (singular)
2. Did you make _that_ pie? (singular)
3. How did he guess _those_ answers? (plural)
4. _These_ toys belong to Katie. (plural)
5. I bought _that_ little red car. (singular)
6. Did you write _these_ stories? (plural)

B. 1. Elle aime bien _ce_ stylo rouge. (masculine, singular)
2. Tu n'aimes pas _cette_ cassette? (feminine, singular)
3. Nous préférons _ces_ tee-shirts bleus. (masculine, plural)
4. Pauline adore _ce_ disque compact. (masculine, singular)
5. Il n'achète pas _ce_ short gris. (masculine, singular)
6. Vous aimez _ces_ montres? (feminine, plural)

C. 1. ce
2. ces
3. cette
4. ces
5. ces
6. cet
7. cette

D. Answers will vary. Possible answer:
Une cassette can refer to any cassette in general. **La cassette** refers to a specific cassette. **Cette cassette** refers to _this_ or _that_ cassette.

Answers

■ ADJECTIVE AGREEMENT AND PLACEMENT

A. 1. Donna has a cute brother with big, blue eyes.
2. The huge locomotive made a loud noise.
3. Our server spilled icy beverages on the clean floor.
4. Does Estéban know the secret combination?
5. He reads a lot of exciting mysteries.

B. 1. Vous aimez cette calculatrice grise?
2. Il me faut trois cahiers jaunes.
3. Sarah achète ces classeurs rouges.
4. J'aime mieux les stylos bleus.
5. C'est combien, ce portefeuille marron?
6. Ils ont des stylos rouges.
7. Il a une maison blanche.

C. Answers will vary. Possible answers:
1. Je voudrais une montre rouge.
2. Tu as un sac noir?
3. Mylène n'a pas d'odinateur violet.
4. Vous aimez cette trousse bleue?
5. Il adore ce sweat-shirt jaune.
6. Tu as des baskets noires?

D. Answers will vary. Possible answer:
In the English sentences, the adjectives are in front of the nouns they describe. In the French sentences, they are placed after the nouns they describe.

CHAPITRE 4

■ QUESTION FORMATION

A. 1. Are you going to lunch at noon?
2. Does she like ice skating and skiing?
3. Is it cold outside?
4. Do they live in Miami, Florida?
5. Will you play tennis with me?
6. Does she like to go to the movies?

B. 1. Est-ce que tu aimes nager?
2. Est-ce qu'Hervé fait du patin?
3. Est-ce que Lucie joue au golf?
4. Est-ce qu'ils voyagent à Paris?
5. Est-ce qu'on fait de l'aérobic?
6. Est-ce que vous faites une promenade?
7. Est-ce qu'il pleut?
8. Est-ce qu'il fait froid en automne?

C. Answers will vary. Possible answers:
Similarities: In both languages, you can raise the pitch of your voice to change a statement into a question.
Differences: In French you can add **est-ce que;** in English you can add **do** or **does.**

■ THE VERB FAIRE

A. Answers may vary. Possible answers:
1. play/are playing
2. do
3. makes
4. play
5. going
6. play

B. 1. action verb: jog or go jogging
2. to do or action verb: act
3. to do
4. to make
5. to play
6. to do or action verb: to take photos

C. 1. fais
2. faire
3. fais
4. faisons
5. font

D. Answers will vary. Possible answer:
The answer to a question containing the verb **faire** may or may not contain a form of **faire.** Examples: **Je fais de la vidéo. Je nage.**

■ ADVERBS

A. 1. She quietly tiptoed up the stairs.
2. You can truly imagine what life was like in the 1800s.
3. I always read the newspaper in the morning.
4. This sauce is too spicy.
5. Do you sometimes think about going to Europe?
6. He was really surprised about the party.

Answers

B. 1. Tu (joues) quelquefois au football?
2. Est-ce qu'il (fait) souvent froid?
3. Je (parle) rarement au téléphone.
4. D'habitude, nous (faisons) du camping.
5. Il ne (neige) jamais en été.
6. De temps en temps, Corinne (fait) du théâtre.
7. Ils (font) du jogging deux fois par semaine.

C. Answers will vary. Possible answers:
1. Je fais la vaisselle trois fois par semaine.
2. Je ne fais jamais d'aérobic.
3. Je joue souvent au football.
4. Je joue quelquefois au tennis
5. Je fais les devoirs de temps en temps.
6. Je fais rarement de la vidéo.
7. Je joue souvent aux cartes.

D. Answers will vary. Possible answer:
Similarities: In both English and French, the placement of adverbs varies.
Differences: In French, some adverbs belong at the beginning of a sentence, while others belong at the end and still others are placed after the word they modify. In English, the same adverb can go at the beginning of a sentence, at the end, or *before* the word it modifies.

CHAPITRE 5

■ THE IMPERATIVE

A. 1. Q
2. S
3. I
4. I
5. Q
6. I
7. Q
8. I

B. 1. Ecoute ce CD!
2. Est-ce que tu as une montre?
3. Donnez-moi un sandwich!
4. Il est cinq heures.
5. On va au café? *or* On va au café.
6. Prends un steak-frites!
7. Nous faisons une promenade.
8. Allons au cinéma!

C. Answers will vary. Possible answers:
1. Etudiez!
2. Prenez une eau minérale!
3. Faites une promenade!
4. Prenez un sandwich!

D. Answers will vary. Possible answer:
1. Prends un sandwich!
2. Ecoute ce disque compact!
3. Fais de la natation!
4. Prends une eau minérale!

E. Answers will vary. Possible answer:
The verb form **regardes** changes to **regarde** when it becomes a command. This happens because you drop the final **-s** from the **tu** form of **-er** verbs in commands.

CHAPITRE 6

■ DAYS OF THE WEEK

A. 1. one specific day
2. regularly
3. regularly
4. one specific day
5. regularly
6. one specific day

B. 1. one specific day
2. regularly
3. one specific day
4. regularly
5. one specific day
6. regularly

C. Answers will vary. Possible answers:
1. Le lundi, je vais au centre commercial.
2. Le mardi, je fais une promenade.
3. Le vendredi, je vais au cinéma.
4. Le samedi, nous allons au théâtre.
5. Vendredi, je vais aller au théâtre.
6. Samedi, je vais aller voir un match de football.
7. Dimanche, je vais faire les vitrines.
8. Mardi, je vais étudier avec Jean-Pierre.

D. Answers will vary. Possible answer:
In French, days of the week are not capitalized.

Answers

■ THE NEAR FUTURE

A. 1. near future
2. near future
3. where
4. near future
5. where

B. 1. where
2. where
3. near future
4. near future
5. near future

C. 1. Michèle ne va pas prendre un coca.
2. Tu vas avoir beaucoup de devoirs.
3. Ils vont aller au musée.
4. Vous allez faire les vitrines dimanche?
5. Nous allons regarder un film samedi.
6. Je vais jouer au tennis.

D. Answers will vary. Possible answers:
1. Je vais aller à l'école.
2. Je vais faire les devoirs.
3. Je vais aller à la piscine.
4. Je vais nager.
5. Je vais regarder un film.

E. Answers will vary. Possible answer:
Item number 1 (**Michèle ne va pas pren-dre un coca.**) is negative. **Ne... pas** goes around the conjugated form of **aller: va.**

■ USING CONTRACTIONS

A. 1. You shouldn't just play all day.
2. He's going to be very pleased.
3. I've got a secret.
4. We don't know whether the story's true or not.
5. I can't tell if she's crying or laughing.
6. He doesn't understand the assignment.

B. 1. Vous allez au stade?
2. Micheline ne va pas à l'université. (no contraction with **à**, but **l'université** is one.)
3. Mes amis parlent au téléphone.
4. Lucie aime jouer aux cartes.
5. Nous adorons aller à la plage. (no contraction)
6. Les élèves vont au centre commercial.

C. 1. à la
2. aux
3. à la
4. au
5. à l'
6. au

D. Answers will vary. Possible answers:
Nous allons au cinéma contains a contraction of **à** and **le (au). J'adore le ciné-ma** contains a contraction of **je** and **adore.** This contraction is made to aid pronuncia-tion. In some French contractions, such as **au** and **aux,** no apostrophe is used.

■ INFORMATION QUESTIONS

A. 1. What is going on?
2. When does summer vacation begin?
3. Why doesn't she call me back?
4. What time is it?
5. How did you do that?
6. Who is at the door?

B. 1. Et demain, tu veux faire quoi?
2. Tu vas au zoo avec qui?
3. Quand est-ce que la bibliothèque ferme?
4. Qu'est-ce que tu veux faire?
5. Où est-ce qu'on va maintenant?
6. Le film commence à quelle heure?
7. Avec qui est-ce que tu vas au cinéma?

C. 1. Quand? / Quand ça?
2. Où? / Où ça?
3. Avec qui?

D. Answers will vary. Possible answer:
A short answer to a similar English ques-tion would not necessarily contain a prepo-sition:
–At what time (When) do we eat lunch?
–(At) Eleven thirty.

ANSWERS

Answers

CHAPITRE 7

■ POSSESSION

A. 1. Don't pull the <u>cat's</u> tail!
   2. Is that <u>Bob's</u> cat?
   3. That's <u>our neighbors'</u> newspaper.
   4. Would you mind closing the <u>principal's</u> door?
   5. The <u>book's</u> binding is cracked.
   6. The <u>teacher's</u> book fell to the floor.
   7. The hands <u>of</u> the clock are broken.

B. 1. Voilà le livre <u>du</u> professeur.
   2. Elle aime bien la cousine <u>de</u> Philippe.
   3. Tu as la montre <u>d'</u>Isabelle?
   4. Ce sont les petits-enfants <u>des</u> voisins <u>de</u> Sophie.
   5. C'est le chien <u>de la</u> fille <u>de</u> Maxime.
   6. J'ai des livres <u>du</u> professor.

C. 1. de
   2. des
   3. du
   4. de l'
   5. de la
   6. d'

D. Answers will vary. Possible answers:
   Similarities: Both French and English show possession using a preposition, **de** in French and **of** in English.
   Differences: In English, **'s** indicates possession. French does not use **'s.** In French, the preposition **de** sometimes combines with other words to form contractions. The English preposition **of** does not combine with other words to form a contraction.

■ POSSESSIVE ADJECTIVES

A. 1. The Smiths bought <u>their</u> first house last month.
   2. <u>His</u> hamster is sleeping in <u>its</u> nest.
   3. Where did I put <u>my</u> keys?
   4. You've finished <u>your</u> chores already?
   5. It's great to hear that <u>our</u> soccer team won.

B. 1. <u>Sa</u> sœur est très mignonne.
   2. <u>Leurs</u> enfants sont pénibles.
   3. Range <u>ta</u> chambre!
   4. <u>Votre</u> fils a deux ans?
   5. Nous faisons <u>nos</u> devoirs maintenant.
   6. C'est une photo de <u>ma</u> grand-mère.
   7. Il n'a pas <u>son</u> cahier.

C. Je vous présente **ma** famille. J'ai un frère. Je n'ai pas de sœur. **Mon** frère s'appelle Frédéric. Il a un chat. **Son** chat s'appelle Lou-Lou. **Nos** parents s'appellent Lucie et Georges. Ils ont deux poissons rouges. **Leurs** poissons s'appellent Plif et Plouf. Et toi, tu as un chien, n'est-ce pas? Comment s'appelle **ton** chien?

D. Answers will vary. Possible answer:
   Son frère can mean **his brother** or **her brother. Sa sœur** can mean his sister or her sister. **Ses cousins** can mean **his cousins** or **her cousins.** In the third person, English possessive adjectives match the gender of the possessor. In French, they match the gender of the person or object possessed.

Answers

CHAPITRE 8

■ PARTITIVE AND INDEFINITE ARTICLES

A. 1. Bring us some water, please.
2. Does Casey have a car?
3. We don't have any milk.
4. She ate an apple and a sandwich.
5. Marie bought some grapes and a melon.
6. I'm afraid he doesn't have any money.

B. 1. Je voudrais du pain, s'il vous plaît. (partitive)
2. Vous avez des haricots verts? (indefinite)
3. Il me faut un avocat. (indefinite)
4. Tu ne prends pas de sucre? (partitive)
6. Prenez de la glace! (partitive)

C. 1. des, du
2. des
3. de
4. du, de la
5. du
6. de
7. une
8. des, du, du

D. Answers will vary. Possible answer:
Use a partitive article to talk about some of something or part of something. Use an indefinite article to talk about the whole thing or more than one thing you can count.

■ THE PRONOUN EN

A. Answers will vary. Possible answers:
1. Yes, I'll bring you some.
2. No, I don't want any.
3. Yes, she did.
4. No, I do not have any.
5. Yes, he wants some.
6. No, they haven't had any. / Yes, they had some.

B. 1. Vous ↓ voulez du fromage.
2. Elle ↓ mange de la pizza.
3. Brigitte et Louise ↓ ont un kilo de pommes.
4. Le marché n'↓ a pas de petits pois.
5. Pierre ↓ achète trois tartes.
6. Je ↓ veux de la farine.
7. Le serveur ↓ apporte une bouteille d'eau minérale.

C. Answers will vary. Possible answers:
1. Oui, j'en prends.
2. Oui, elle en achète.
3. Oui, nous en avons deux bouteilles.
4. Non, je n'en veux pas.
5. Non, je n'en ai pas besoin.
6. Si, j'en ai.

D. Answers will vary. Possible answers:
1. In the first conversation, the pronoun **en** means *of it.*
2. In the second conversation, the pronoun **en** means *any.*

ANSWERS

Answers

CHAPITRE 9

■ THE PAST TENSE

A. 1. Carlos and Rita <u>ordered</u> soup and salad.
2. My grandmother <u>worked</u> at the grocery store.
3. The kitten <u>hid</u> inside the sack.
4. Her older brother <u>drove</u> to school.
5. Who <u>brought</u> the balloons?
6. We <u>visited</u> my grandmother many times.
7. She <u>came</u> to see us every Christmas.

B. 1. Qu'est-ce que tu (as) fait ce week-end?
2. Nous (avons) vu un film.
3. J'(ai) mangé de la pizza.
4. Claire (a) étudié à la bibliothèque.
5. Ils (ont) pris un taxi.
6. Vous (avez) gagné le match de hockey?
7. Les élèves (ont) visité le musée.

C. 1. Vous avez lavé la voiture.
2. Séverine a pris le déjeuner au café.
3. Tu as lu un bon livre.
4. Ils ont fait un pique-nique au parc.
5. Je n'ai pas parlé au téléphone.
6. Nous avons mangé la pizza.

D. Answers will vary. Possible answer:
In the present, **ne... pas** goes around the verb. In the near future, **ne... pas** goes around the first verb (a form of **aller**). In the past, **ne... pas** goes around the helping verb.

Answers

CHAPITRE 10

■ DIRECT OBJECTS

A. 1. The store also lends tapes.
2. Her parents drive an antique car.
3. Margie lit a candle.
4. I'm meeting George at the park.
5. Brandon studies French and Latin.
6. The dog always obeys his master.
7. She doesn't understand the lesson.

B. 1. Tu as ton sac?
2. Il apporte son manteau.
3. Vous prenez cette chemise?
4. J'ai mis une robe.
5. Delphine veut essayer ces bottes.
6. Philippe n'aime pas cette cravate.
7. Elles trouvent ces sandales un peu démodées.

C. Answers will vary. Possible answers:
1. J'aime bien le chocolat.
2. Comment tu trouves cette robe?
3. Nous avons pris nos livres.
4. Au magasin, Magali choisit le pantalon noir.
5. Pour aller à une boum, Mireille met sa veste violette.
6. Tu vas acheter cet ordinateur?

D. Answers will vary. Possible answer:
The sentence **J'aime le chocolat** has a direct object because **le chocolat** comes right after the verb. In the second sentence, the preposition **à** comes before **l'école,** so it does not have a direct object.

■ DIRECT OBJECT PRONOUNS

A. 1. it
2. it
3. them
4. them
5. it
6. them
7. them

B. 1. la; l' before acheter
2. le
3. les
4. les
5. le
6. le; l' before aimer

C. Answers will vary. Possible answers:
1. Non, je ne les aime pas.
2. Oui, je le prends.
3. Si, je l'aime.
4. Je la trouve moche.
5. Si, je l'ai.
6. Oui, je la préfère.

D. Answers will vary. Possible answer:
In the present, **ne... pas** goes around the verb and the pronoun. In the past, **ne... pas** goes around the helping verb and the pronoun. In the near future, **ne... pas** goes around the first verb (a form of **aller**) and before the pronoun.

Answers

CHAPITRE 11

■ PREPOSITIONS WITH GEOGRAPHICAL PLACE NAMES

A. 1. to
2. to
3. in
4. in
5. to
6. to
7. in

B. 1. Stéphane voudrait aller au Canada. (to)
2. Tu as un frère qui habite à Londres? (in)
3. Mes amis ont passé un week-end en Allemagne. (in)
4. Je suis allé à la Martinique. (to)
5. Nons prenons le train pour aller en Espagne. (to)
6. A Paris, il y a beaucoup de musées. (in)
7. Elle va aller au Brésil. (to)
8. Son oncle habite aux Etats-Unis. (in)

C. 1. aux
2. en
3. au
4. au
5. à/au
6. en, en
7. en
8. au

D. Answers will vary. Possible answer:
Feminine countries end in **-e. Le Mexique**
also ends in **-e,** but it is masculine.

Answers

CHAPITRE 12

■ THE PRONOUN Y

A. 1. Mom's at the store.
2. I can't wait to go to San Diego.
3. John and Julie are in Colorado.
4. Her best friend is moving to Seattle.
5. The State Fair takes place in Dallas.
6. They go to France often.

B. 1. Maman va au supermarché le lundi.
2. Est-ce qu'on peut aller à la piscine cet après-midi?
3. Laure fait de l'athlétisme au stade.
4. Didier et Thomas vont au cinéma avec Pauline et Marithé.
5. Cécile est allée à Berlin l'été dernier.
6. Tu vas au lycée le samedi matin?
7. Nons prenons le bus pour aller au centre commercial.

C. 1. Maman y va le lundi.
2. Est-ce qu'on peut y aller cet après-midi?
3. Laure y fait de l'athlétisme.
4. Didier et Thomas y vont avec Pauline et Marithé.
5. Cécile y est allée l'été dernier.
6. Tu y vas le samedi matin?
7. Nons prenons le bus pour y aller.

D. Answers will vary. Possible answer:
The placement of the pronoun **y** is similar to the placement of other object pronouns. In the present, both **y** and **le, la, les,** or **l'** go before the verb.
J'y vais. Je l'achète.
In the past, both **y** and **le, la, les,** or **l'** go before the helping verb.
J'y suis allé. Je l'ai acheté.
In the near future, both **y** and **le, la, les,** or **l'** go before the second verb.
Je vais y aller. Je vais l'acheter.

■ USING CONTRACTIONS

A. 1. doesn't
2. can't
3. I'm
4. They're
5. Mary's
6. didn't

B. 1. Sur cette photo, Michèle est à côté du père de Sylvie.
2. La bibliothèque est en face de la gare. (no contraction – leave as is)
3. C'est tout de suite à droite, devant le cinéma. (no contraction – leave as is)
4. La pharmacie est loin du café.
5. Le Mexique est près des Etats-Unis.
6. La boulangerie est au coin de la rue. (no contraction – leave as is)

C. 1. de la
2. du
3. de la
4. du
5. des
6. de l'
7. de la

D. Answers will vary. Possible answer:
Not all expressions that give a location require a preposition. Words like **derrière, entre,** and **devant** are followed directly by the place name without **de la, du, des,** or **de l'.**

Allez, viens! French 2

Answers

Answers

CHAPITRE 1

■ INTERROGATIVE ADJECTIVES

A.
1. <u>What</u> fell off the shelf?
2. <u>What</u> is the problem?
3. <u>Which</u> course is Lola taking?
4. <u>What</u> did Frank buy at the mall?
5. <u>Which</u> one is the best?
6. <u>What</u> is the address here?

B.
1. Quels
2. Quel
3. Quelles
4. Quel
5. Quelle
6. Quel
7. Quelle
8. Quel

C.
1. Quel
2. Qu'est-ce que

D. Answers will vary. Possible answers:
1. In this sentence, the missing word is followed by a form of the verb **être**. Since it goes with the noun **sport**, the question word is an adjective (a form of **quel**). Since **sport** is masculine and singular, the correct form is **quel**.
2. In this sentence, the missing word is not followed by a form of the verb **être**. Because the subject and verb are already present in the sentence, the missing word is the direct object. The question word that can stand for a direct object is **qu'est-ce que**.

Answers

CHAPITRE 2

■ ADJECTIVE PLACEMENT

A. 1. Sandy bought a pretty green skirt.
2. My neighbor has a black dog.
3. Alex has never seen a foreign movie.
4. I'd like a nice cold glass of water.
5. The first-grade students loved listening to fairy tales.

B. 1. Sophie a une voiture bleue.
2. Ils ont un chien méchant.
3. Les Morgan ont une grande maison.
4. La chanteuse a chanté une belle chanson.
5. Ma cousine aime les vieux films.
6. Christelle n'a pas de chaussures rouges.

C. 1. Monique préfère les jeans noirs.
2. Nous avons une vieille voiture.
3. Tu aimes leur nouvelle cassette?
4. Le petit garçon a trouvé son chat.
5. Ma tante habite dans une belle ville.
6. Je suis allé dans un restaurant cher.
7. Tu as des amis sympathiques.

D. Answers will vary. Possible answers:
1. Like most adjectives, **moderne** belongs after the noun.
2. The adjective **grande** belongs before the noun.
3. When you have more than one adjective, each one follows its own placement rule, so **grande** goes before the noun and **moderne** goes after it.

Answers

CHAPITRE 3

■ INDIRECT OBJECT PRONOUNS

A. 1. Gabriel's friend showed him some other sights.
2. Did your dad teach you those magic tricks?
3. Let's write our congresswoman a letter.
4. Sam made us a table in shop class.
5. Save me a place in line.

B. 1. Tu pourrais offrir un CD à Sophie.
2. Je dois téléphoner à mes parents.
3. Est-ce que vous pouvez donner un livre à Jean-Marc?
4. Le prof d'histoire va rendre les devoirs aux élèves.
5. Nous pouvons parler à Mylène et François.
6. Mon frère va donner une boîte de chocolats à sa copine.
7. Ma tante offre toujours des bonbons à mes parents.

C. 1. lui
2. leur
3. lui
4. leur
5. leur
6. lui
7. leur

D. Answers will vary. Possible answers: Similarities: In three of the four sentences, the indirect object goes after the verb. Differences: In French, indirect object pronouns belong before the verb.

Answers

CHAPITRE 4

■ RELATIVE PRONOUNS: *CE QUI* AND *CE QUE*

A. 1. object
2. subject
3. object
4. object
5. subject

B. 1. Ce qu'
2. Ce qui
3. Ce que
4. Ce que
5. Ce que
6. Ce qui
7. Ce qu'

C. Answers will vary. Possible answers:
1. Ce que j'aime, c'est danser
2. Ce qui me plaît, c'est de me promener dans le parc.
3. Ce que je préfère, c'est la pizza.
4. Ce qui m'amuse, c'est les zoos.
5. Ce que je n'aime pas, c'est les asperges.
6. Ce qui m'ennuie, c'est de jouer au golf.

D. Answers will vary. Possible answers:
1. In this sentence, the missing pronoun is the object of the verb **dit**, so the correct relative pronoun is **ce que**.
2. In this sentence, the missing pronoun is the subject of the verb **plaît**, so the correct pronoun is **ce qui**.

■ REFLEXIVE VERBS

A. 1. non-reflexive
2. reflexive
3. reflexive
4. non-reflexive
5. reflexive
6. non-reflexive

B. 1. reflexive
2. non-reflexive
3. reflexive
4. reflexive
5. non-reflexive
6. non-reflexive
7. reflexive
8. reflexive

C. 1. Ma cousine se couche à 11h00.
2. Tu t'amuses bien ce soir?
3. Nous nous promenons dans les montagnes.
4. Gilles et Claire se lèvent à 7h30.
5. On se baigne tous les jours.
6. Vous vous ennuyez chez vos grands-parents?
7. Combien de fois par jour est-ce qu'il se brosse les dents?
8. Je me lave le matin avant le petit-déjeuner.

D. Answers will vary. Possible answer: Reflexive pronouns match the subjects: **me** goes with **je**, **te** goes with **tu**, and so on.

Answers

CHAPITRE 5

■ IRREGULAR PAST PARTICIPLES

A. 1. begun
2. froze
3. known
4. eaten
5. driven
6. did

B. 1. as
2. ai
3. ont
4. ont
5. avez
6. a
7. avons

C. 1. regardé
2. pris
3. rencontré
4. vu
5. bu
6. été
7. fait

D. Answers will vary. Possible answer:
In the passé composé, **ne... pas** goes around the helping verb. In the sentence "Il n'a pas joué au tennis." the verb **a** begins with a vowel, so **ne** becomes **n'**.

Answers

CHAPITRE 6

■ THE PAST TENSE WITH ÊTRE

A.
1. have admired
2. has dropped
3. has worn
4. has sung
5. have broken

B.
1. es
2. avons
3. sont
4. sont
5. as
6. est
7. avez

C.
1. arrivée
2. montés
3. X
4. X
5. descendue
6. X
7. retournées

D. Answers will vary. Possible answer: This sentence refers to a mixed group (male and female) of people. The **-s** is added because because the subject is plural.

Answers

CHAPITRE 7

■ REFLEXIVE VERBS IN THE PAST

A. 1. She
2. They
3. We
4. He
5. I

B. 1. g
2. e
3. f
4. d
5. a
6. b
7. c

C. Answers will vary. Possible answers:
1. Je ne me suis pas promené(e) en ville.
2. Je me suis couché(e) tard.
3. Tony s'est cassé la jambe.
4. Laura s'est levée à 7h30.
5. Don s'est fait mal.
6. Je me suis brossé les dents trois fois par jour.
7. Nous nous sommes amusé(e)s samedi soir.

D. Answers will vary. Possible answer:
In the second sentence, the past participle does not agree with the subject because the object **les cheveux**, not the subject **elle**, receives the action of the verb.

■ THE PRONOUN EN

A. Answers will vary. Possible answers:
1. The children did the dishes after dinner.
2. We played games.
3. They made the cake for her birthday.
4. Will you make some cookies?
5. Can you play that song?

B. Answers will vary. Possible answers:
1. Richard fait de la planche à voile tous les samedis.
2. Nous prenons souvent des croissants au petit-déjeuner.
3. Je ne mange pas de poulet.
4. Elle ne veut pas de riz.
5. M. et Mme Chambord achètent des fruits au marché.

C. Answers will vary. Possible answers:
1. Je la fais souvent.
2. Je n'en fais jamais.
3. J'en fais rarement.
4. Je la fais de temps en temps.
5. J'en fais quelquefois.
6. Je n'en fais jamais.
7. Je les fais souvent.
8. J'en fais rarement.

D. Answers will vary. Possible answer:
The pronoun **en** replaces nouns preceded by **du, de la,** and so on, so it could stand for **du piano** in sentence b. **En** cannot replace a noun after **aux**, so it could not work in sentence a.

Answers

CHAPITRE 8

■ THE IMPERFECT

A. 1. They used to walk to school together.
2. It was raining and the wind was blowing.
3. We used to spend every summer at the beach.
4. Sylvia was running late to her appointment.
5. Mrs. Brown would give us cookies after school.
6. Thirty minutes later, the food was getting cold.

B. 1. Nous faisions souvent du ski en hiver.
2. Tu promenais ton chien?
3. Je prenais mon déjeuner à midi.
4. Mylène et Caroline avaient soif.
5. Vous étiez très fatigués.
6. Il faisait frais hier soir.
7. On allait toujours au cinéma le vendredi.

C. 1. Je lisais des bandes dessinées.
2. Nous allions au supermarché le dimanche.
3. Bruno et Sylvie habitaient à la campagne.
4. Tu promenais ton chien après l'école?
5. On avait très soif.
6. Ma sœur sortait la poubelle le vendredi.

D. Answers will vary. Possible answer:
The stems are different because you need to add an **-e** before the ending **-ais** to keep the **g** sound the same (like the **s** in treasure, not like the **g** as in go). In the second sentence, you don't need to add **-e** before the ending **-iez**.

Answers

CHAPITRE 9

■ THE PAST TENSE: *PASSÉ COMPOSÉ VS THE IMPARFAIT*

A. 1. completed event
2. regularly occurring event
3. completed event
4. ongoing condition or activity
5. ongoing condition or activity
6. completed event

B. 1. Il <u>faisait</u> toujours beau le matin. (ongoing condition)
2. Jean <u>était</u> inquiet. (ongoing condition)
3. Je <u>n'ai pas fait</u> la vaisselle hier soir. (completed event)
4. D'habitude, j'<u>allais</u> au café avec mes copains. (regular event)
5. David <u>a pris</u> un lait fraise. (completed event)
6. Odile <u>a eu</u> une bonne note en histoire. (completed event)
7. Tu <u>étais</u> de mauvaise humeur cet après-midi. (ongoing condition)

C. 1. est allé
2. ai eu
3. faisait
4. prenions
5. arrivait
6. est tombée
7. alliez
8. arrêtions

D. Answers will vary. Possible answer: Words like **soudain** and **d'abord** refer to a specific moment in the past, so they would be used in the **passé composé**. Words like **souvent** or **tous les jours** refer to repeated actions, so they would be used in the **imparfait**.

Answers

CHAPITRE 10

■ OBJECT PRONOUNS AND THEIR PLACEMENT

A. 1. Would you like the band to play a song for you?
2. We never did bring you any flowers.
3. He called me last evening.

B. 1. Elle l'a vu au restaurant.
2. Tu leur as parlé?
3. Je vous invite chez moi ce soir.
4. Excusez-moi!
5. Tu ne veux pas me parler?
6. Je te présente mon père.
7. Il nous a demandé pardon.

C. 1. Oui, il va les voir cet été.
2. Oui, je peux t'aider à faire la vaisselle.
3. Non, je ne vous ai pas invités pas chez moi ce week-end.
4. Non, je ne voudrais pas vous acheter ce disque compact.
5. Oui, je lui ai donné un cadeau pour son anniversaire.
6. Oui, tu peux me parler.
7. Nous allons leur téléphoner.

D. Answers will vary. Possible answers:
1. The past participle **invités** has an **-s** on the end because the direct object pronoun **les** stands for **amis**, which is plural.
2. The past participle **vue** has an **-e** on the end because the direct object pronoun **l'** stands for **soeur**, which is feminine.
3. The past participle **parlé** has no **-e** on the end because the pronoun **lui** stands for an indirect object. Past participles agree with direct object pronouns, not indirect object pronouns.

Answers

CHAPITRE 11

■ IDENTIFYING AND DESCRIBING PEOPLE

A. 1. X
2. a
3. a
4. an
5. a
6. X

B. 1. une
2. X
3. X
4. une
5. X
6. X
7. un

C. 1. C'est
2. Elle est
3. C'est
4. Il est
5. C'est
6. Il est
7. Elle est
8. C'est

D. Answers will vary. Possible answers:
1. You use indefinite articles with nouns, but you don't use an article with an adjective alone.
2. Nationalities that begin with capital letters are nouns. Adjectives of nationality are not capitalized.

■ RELATIVE PRONOUNS: *QUI AND QUE*

A. 1. Linda is a friend <u>whom</u> I trust. (direct object)
2. Billy read from a book <u>that</u> he wrote. (direct object)
3. Mrs. Franklin gave me a toy <u>that</u> glows in the dark. (subject)
4. The lightbulb <u>which</u> had been flickering finally burned out. (subject)
5. That was a movie <u>that</u> we really enjoyed. (direct object)

B. 1. C'est un film <u>que</u> je n'aime pas. (direct object, thing)
2. Louise est une amie <u>qui</u> est sincère. (subject, person)
3. Voici l'arbre <u>qui</u> est tombé sur notre maison. (subject, thing)
4. La pièce <u>que</u> vous avez vue était bonne? (direct object, thing)
5. Francis est un homme <u>qui</u> est devenu architecte. (subject, person)
6. C'est l'histoire d'une fille <u>qui</u> habite à Nice. (subject, person)
7. Jocelyne est la dame <u>que</u> j'ai connue à Marseille. (direct object, person)

C. 1. qu'
2. qui
3. que
4. que
5. qui
6. qui
7. qui
8. que

D. Answers will vary. Possible answer: There is an **-es** on the end of **faites** because when the **passé composé** comes after **que**, the past participle agrees with whatever **que** stands for. In this sentence, **que** stands for **tartes**, which is feminine and plural.

Answers

CHAPITRE 12

■ ADVERBS WITH THE PAST TENSE

A.
1. Laura went to the store <u>yesterday</u>. (completed event)
2. <u>Suddenly</u>, the phone rang. (completed event)
3. It <u>usually</u> rained when I washed my car. (regularly occurring event or condition)
4. I <u>once</u> caught a fish. (completed event)
5. <u>One day</u>, a letter arrived from my cousin. (completed event)
6. The choir <u>often</u> sang at weddings. (regularly occurring event or condition)

B.
1. J'allais <u>souvent</u> au cinéma. (regularly occurring event or condition)
2. <u>De temps en temps</u>, il faisait du camping. (regularly occurring event or condition)
3. <u>Un jour</u>, ma cousine est arrivée. (completed event)
4. <u>D'habitude</u>, mon père était de bonne humeur. (regularly occurring event or condition)
5. Il pleuvait <u>toujours</u> au printemps. (regularly occurring event or condition)
6. <u>D'abord</u>, on a visité le musée de beaux arts. (completed event)
7. <u>Soudain</u>, j'ai eu une idée. (completed event)

C. Answers will vary. Possible answers:
1. Soudain, j'ai vu mon amie, Sarah.
2. Un jour, ma famille a eu un accident de voiture.
3. D'abord, on est allé au restaurant.
4. D'habitude, mon professeur était sympa.
5. De temps en temps, mes amis jouaient au football.
6. Ils faisaient souvent du canotage.
7. Une fois, tu lui as donné un cadeau pour son anniversaire.
8. Le dimanche, nous visitions les monuments.

D. Answers will vary. Possible answers:
1. The adverb **souvent** tells that the event occurred *often*. Also, the definite article in **le samedi matin** indicates that it occurred *every* Saturday morning.
2. The adverbs **d'abord** and **ensuite** tell the order of single, completed events that occurred.

Allez, viens! French 3

Answers

Answers

CHAPITRE 1

▇ THE PAST TENSE

A. 1. Carl (has) written a letter to his congress-man.
2. Fred married my sister.
3. Who let the cat in?
4. I (have) seen this movie before.
5. Cheryl (has)n't received her invitation yet.
6. The newspaper arrived late again today.

B. 1. Francine s'(est) réveillée à six heures.
2. Paulette (a) mangé une pomme.
3. Tu (as) mis une cravate ce soir!
4. La pauvre Nanette (est) tombée d'un arbre.
5. Les Granger (ont) eu un accident de voiture.
6. J'(ai) fini tous mes devoirs avant huit heures.
7. Nous (sommes) restés chez Tante Huguette.

C. 1. a
2. ont
3. es
4. suis
5. a
6. a
7. avons
8. êtes

D. Answers will vary. Possible answer:
In the first sentence, the past participle agrees with the subject because the reflexive pronoun (**s'**) is the direct object of the action. In the second sentence, the past participle does not agree with the subject because there is a direct object (**la jambe**).

Answers

CHAPITRE 2

■ PRONOUNS AND THEIR PLACEMENT

A. 1. Frankie threw (me) the ball.
2. Lisa gave (Phil) a big party.
3. Caroline sent (Bobby) a package.
4. Our neighbor brought (us) our newspaper.
5. Lynn taught (her son) Spanish.
6. She sometimes buys (herself) roses.

B. 1. Marie-Laure est allée à San Francisco.
2. Achète cette robe!
3. Ils ont visité le musée.
4. Noémie voudrait trois tranches de jambon.
5. Florent va téléphoner (à ses parents) demain.
6. Tu donnes ton numéro de téléphone (à Lola)?
7. J'ai vu Daria au centre commercial.

C. 1. Marie-Laure y est allée.
2. Achète-la!
3. Ils l'ont visité.
4. Noémie en voudrait trois tranches.
5. Florent va leur téléphoner demain.
6. Tu le lui donnes?
7. Je l'y ai vu.

D. Answers will vary. Possible answer: The indirect object pronoun **me** becomes **moi** in a command. It is placed after the verb with a hyphen.

Answers

CHAPITRE 3

■■ THE SUBJUNCTIVE

A. 1. imperative
2. indicative
3. subjunctive
4. indicative
5. imperative
6. subjunctive

B. 1. indicative
2. subjunctive
3. imperative
4. subjunctive
5. indicative

C. Answers will vary. Possible answer:
All of the subjunctive forms of **prendre** are based on the **ils/elles** form of the indicative except for **nous** and **vous**. The stems of the **nous** and **vous** forms are the same in the indicative and the subjunctive (**pren-**). In both the indicative and the subjunctive, the **ils/elles** form is **prennent**.

Answers

CHAPITRE 4

■ THE INTERROGATIVE AND DEMONSTRATIVE PRONOUNS

A.
1. which one, interrogative
2. those, demonstrative
3. which ones, interrogative
4. this one, demonstrative
5. these, demonstrative

B.
1. celui-là, demonstrative
2. laquelle, interrogative
3. lequel, interrogative
4. ceux-là, demonstrative
5. celles-là, demonstrative

C.
1. celui-là
2. celle-là
3. Celui-là.
4. Lesquelles?
5. Celles-là.
6. Lequel?

D. Answers will vary. Possible answer:
Lequel?
In this sentence, the interrogative pronoun stands for a noun that is masculine and singular, **chat**. The words **il**, **ce**, **petit**, and **mignon** are all in the masculine singular form. The verb **est** shows that it is singular.

Answers

CHAPITRE 5

■ THE FUTURE

A.
1. We will do the dishes after the movie.
2. Dad will be pleased with your grades.
3. I will not stay here past Saturday.
4. Martin won't hesitate to help us.
5. The couple will have a baby this fall.
6. Our team will win the game.

B.
1. Tes amis se marieront.
2. Nous choisirons un métier.
3. Christine entrera à l'université.
4. Je voyagerai beaucoup.
5. Tu iras en Europe.
6. Lise deviendra médecin.
7. Vous verrez le monde.

C.
1. Je deviendrai ingénieur.
2. Thomas fera un long voyage.
3. Tu enverras une lettre à une école technique.
4. Nous choisirons une université.
5. Vous aurez des enfants.
6. Christelle et Olivier se marieront.
7. Nous serons très contents.

D. Answers will vary. Possible answers:

j'ai	nous avons	je choisirai	nous choisirons
tu as	vous avez	tu choisiras	vous choisirez
il as	ils ont	il choisira	ils choisiront

The endings of the future tense are the same as the forms of **avoir** in the present tense, except for **nous** and **vous**. Because I know the forms of **avoir**, the future tense endings should be easy to remember.

■ THE CONDITIONAL

A.
1. She would help you if you asked her to.
2. Joe would buy this bike if it were less expensive.
3. You would look handsome in that suit.
4. Would you like to go to the park?
5. I would love to meet your friends.
6. If they knew him better, they would believe his story.
7. He would never go on a safari.
8. What would you like to do after high school?

B.
1. S'il faisait beau, je jouerais au tennis.
2. Tu pourrais me passer du sel?
3. J'aimerais être avocate.
4. Ça serait super si tu pouvais venir cet été.
5. Mes cousins viendraient plus souvent si nous avions une grande maison.
6. Est-ce que vous voudriez visiter des châteaux?
7. Qu'est-ce que tu ferais à ma place?

C.
1. Si je (tombais / tomberais) amoureux, je me (mariais / marierais).
2. Nous (cherchions / chercherions) un emploi, si nous (étions / serions) au chômage.
3. Si mes parents (gagnaient / gagneraient) plus d'argent, nous (voyagions / voyagerions).
4. S'ils (avaient / auraient) un enfant, ils (avaient / auraient) beaucoup de responsabilités.
5. J(e) (étais / serais) dans un groupe de rock, si je (jouais / jouerais) de la guitare.
6. Si elle (réussissait / réussirait) au bac, elle (allait / irait) à l'université.
7. Vous me (téléphoniez / téléphoneriez), si vous (vouliez / voudriez) me parler.

D. Answers will vary. Possible answers:
Je voudrais une glace.
With the verb in the conditional, this sentence becomes a polite request. The first sentence is more like a command than a request.

Answers

CHAPITRE 6

■ RECIPROCAL VERBS

A. 1. Manuel and Robert <u>help</u> <u>each other</u> study for the test.
2. Elisa and Anne <u>argue</u> with <u>each other</u> all the time.
3. Now the girls <u>aren't speaking</u> to <u>one another</u>.
4. They finally <u>made up</u> with <u>each other</u>.
5. We <u>like each other</u>.
6. The family members <u>support</u> <u>one another</u>.
7. Ricardo and Lucy never <u>lie</u> to <u>each other</u>.
8. The students <u>tell</u> <u>one another</u> about their vacation.

B. 1. Nous <u>nous</u> aimons bien.
2. Vous <u>vous</u> disputez trop souvent.
3. Vous <u>vous</u> êtes rencontrés où?
4. Ils <u>se</u> sont offert des cadeaux.
5. Nous <u>nous</u> parlions rarement au lycée.
6. Ils <u>se</u> sont regardés et tout de suite, ils se sont plus.
7. Nous ne <u>nous</u> voyons jamais pendant le week-end.
8. Pourquoi Fatima et Alice <u>se</u> sont disputées?

C. 1. Nous nous sommes vu(e)s dimanche.
2. Julie et Jean se sont retrouvés à la piscine.
3. Carole et Charlotte se sont réconciliées.
4. Est-ce que Georges et toi, vous vous êtes beaucoup aimés?
5. Nous nous sommes dit la vérité.
6. Elles se sont parlé aussi souvent que possible.

D. Answers will vary. Possible answers:
1. The verb **voir** has no preposition before its object, so it is direct.
2. **Téléphoner** is followed by the preposition **à**, so its object, Pam, is indirect.

Answers

CHAPITRE 7

■ USING THE SUBJUNCTIVE

A. 1. subjunctive
2. indicative
3. subjunctive
4. subjunctive
5. indicative
6. subjunctive

B. 1. indicative
2. subjunctive
3. subjunctive
4. indicative
5. indicative
6. subjunctive

C. Answers will vary. Possible answers:
1. Je suis certain qu'il viendra ce soir.
2. Il faudrait que tu arrives à l'heure.
3. Il n'est pas sûr qu'elle soit ici.
4. Il se peut qu'il fasse très froid.
5. Nous savons que vous êtes fatigué.
6. Il est essentiel que tu restes à la maison.
7. Je suis désolé que tu ne puisse pas venir.

D. Answers will vary. Possible answer:
The verb in the sentence «**Je pense qu'il est gentil**» is in the indicative mood because the speaker is fairly certain of what he or she is saying. «**Je ne pense pas qu'il soit méchant**» is in the subjunctive because it expresses doubt.

CHAPITRE 8

■ THE COMPARATIVE

A. 1. My suitcase is <u>heavier than</u> yours. (adjective)
2. This poster is <u>more colorful than</u> that one. (adjective)
3. John ate <u>more pizza than</u> Rachid. (noun)
4. Luis speaks <u>more softly than</u> Rachel. (adverb)
5. They <u>study more than</u> Ellen. (verb)

B. 1. Je chante <u>mieux que</u> Sylvie. (verb)
2. Les gens sont <u>plus pressés</u> à Paris qu'à Reno. (adjective)
3. Il y a <u>plus d'animaux</u> dans la forêt qu'en ville. (noun)
4. L'histoire, c'est <u>plus intéressant que</u> les maths. (adjective)
5. Les cafés sont <u>meilleurs</u> à New York qu'à Dakar. (adjective)
6. Laure <u>nage moins</u> bien <u>que</u> Philippe. (verb)
7. J'ai <u>autant de livres que</u> Michèle. (noun)

C. 1. Cécile s'habille moins bien qu'Yvette.
2. Louise est plus petite que Marc.
3. Elles chantent mieux que moi.
4. Lise a autant d'argent qu'Elisabeth.
5. Vous êtes aussi drôle que Stéphane.
6. Les quiches sont meilleures que la soupe.

D. Answers will vary. Possible answer: There are several forms of **meilleur** because it is an adjective and adjectives agree with the nouns they refer to. There is only one form of **mieux** because adverbs do not change form.

Answers

CHAPITRE 9

NEGATIVE EXPRESSIONS

A. 1. Don does <u>not</u> go <u>anywhere</u> during the week.
2. <u>Nobody</u> brought <u>anything</u> to drink.
3. I like <u>neither</u> spiders <u>nor</u> snakes.
4. <u>Nothing</u> exciting ever happens here.
5. Tina has <u>nothing</u> to give him for his birthday.

B. 1. Je ne fais <u>rien</u> cet aprèm.
2. Elle <u>n'</u>est <u>allée</u> <u>nulle part</u> pendant les vacances.
3. <u>Personne ne</u> sait jouer aux cartes?
4. Délia <u>n'</u>est <u>pas encore</u> arrivée?
5. <u>Rien ne</u> passe à la télé ce soir.
6. Je <u>n'</u>aime <u>ni</u> la chimie <u>ni</u> la biologie.
7. Vous <u>n'</u>avez <u>aucun</u> livre de Saint-Exupéry?

C. 1. Tu ne fais jamais la vaisselle.
2. Karine n'a ni son manteau ni sa casquette.
3. Ils n'ont pas encore fini leurs devoirs.
4. Je ne veux aller nulle part.
5. Rien n'est arrivé la semaine dernière.
6. Il n'y avait personne au supermarché.

D. Answers will vary. Possible answer:
Personne ne goes near the beginning of a sentence and functions as a subject. **Ne... personne** goes around the verb and functions as an adverb.

RELATIVE PRONOUNS

A. 1. Mandy broke the statue <u>that</u> she bought. (object, thing)
2. This is the student for <u>whom</u> I voted. (object, person)
3. I like the flowers ^ she brought me. (object, thing)
4. Jolene is the one <u>who</u> called this morning. (subject, person)
5. I know the boy <u>whom</u> you saw. (object, person)

B. 1. C'est un film <u>qui</u> fait rire. (subject, thing)
2. Nadia est une fille <u>que</u> je connais bien. (object, person)
3. La Guadeloupe est une île <u>dont</u> on rêve. (object, thing)
4. Luc a raconté une histoire <u>que</u> je ne crois pas. (object, thing)
5. J'aime bien le cadeau <u>qu'</u>elle m'a donné. (object, thing)
6. Il est où, le restaurant <u>dont</u> elle t'a parlé? (object, thing)
7. Je me souviens d'un acteur <u>qui</u> est très drôle. (subject, person)

C. 1. Le professeur dont tu m'as parlé est sympa.
2. Où sont les boissons que Maman a achetées?
3. J'aime bien l'hôtel que la concierge a recommandé.
4. J'ai connu la fille qui habite à côté de chez nous.
5. C'est la voiture qui a causé un accident.

D. Answers will vary. Possible answer:
When a relative pronoun is an object, it is usually followed by a noun or a pronoun. In the first sentence, the relative pronoun **que** is followed by the pronoun **je,** which is the subject of the clause. The subject of a clause is usually followed by a verb. For example, the relative pronoun **qui** in the second sentence is followed by the verb **a sauvé**.

Answers

CHAPITRE 10

■ THE SUPERLATIVE

A. 1. Frieda is <u>the kindest</u> person I know. (adjective)
2. It is Paul who writes me <u>the most regularly</u>. (adverb)
3. Of all my friends, Jack <u>talks the most</u>. (verb)
4. Barbara has <u>the least time</u> among all of us. (noun)

B. 1. C'est François qui court <u>le moins vite</u>. (adverb)
2. Kevin et Michel sont mes <u>meilleurs</u> amis. (adjective)
3. Amélie est <u>la</u> fille <u>la plus sage</u> de notre famille. (adjective)
4. C'est Romain qui <u>m'amuse le plus</u>. (verb)
5. C'est dans cette ville qu'il y a <u>le moins de pollution</u>. (noun)
6. Dorothée est l'élève qui travaille <u>le mieux</u>. (adverb)
7. Les Salines est <u>la plus belle</u> plage du monde. (adjective)

C. 1. Toi, tu chantes le mieux.
2. Maryse saute le plus haut.
3. Florence est la moins gentille.
4. Viviane court le moins vite.
5. Christophe et Janine sont les plus sérieux.
6. Nous nous parlons le plus souvent au téléphone.

■ THE PAST PERFECT

A. 1. She <u>had</u> always <u>considered</u> Lois a close friend.
2. They <u>had</u> not <u>forgotten</u> us after all.
3. We <u>had</u> just <u>started</u> to eat when the phone rang.
4. A huge spider <u>had</u> <u>spun</u> a web outside the door.
5. Charlene <u>had</u> never <u>been</u> to a circus before.
6. We <u>had</u> <u>drunk</u> some water before starting the race.

B. 1. Nous <u>avions déménagé</u> en Angleterre.
2. Ils <u>étaient allés</u> en France.
3. J'<u>avais oublié</u> son adresse.
4. Marithé <u>avait téléphoné</u> à Pierre.
5. Christelle <u>s'était fait</u> mal au pied en marchant.
6. Micheline <u>avait</u> vite <u>fait</u> le ménage.

C. 1. être, était
2. avoir, avais
3. avoir, avaient
4. être, étaient
5. être, était
6. avoir, avait

D. 1. était parti
2. s'étaient mariés
3. avais eu
4. avait acheté
5. avions pris
6. avais fait

E. Answers will vary. Possible answer: The first sentence is in the **passé composé**. It means *you left*. The **passé composé** is made up of the present tense of the helping verb and a past participle. The second sentence is in the **plus-que-parfait**. It means *you had left*. The **plus-que-parfait** is made up of the imperfect of the helping verb and a past participle.

Answers

CHAPITRE 11

■ RELATIVE PRONOUNS

A. 1. I don't know <u>what</u> you're talking about. (object)
2. They liked <u>what</u> they saw in Rome. (object)
3. <u>What</u>'s interesting is the color of this house. (subject)
4. They don't know <u>what</u>'s best for them. (subject)
5. I'll tell you <u>what</u> she likes. (object)
6. No one knows <u>what</u> will happen next. (subject)

B. 1. <u>Ce que</u> je mange, c'est du jambalaya. (object)
2. Je ne sais pas <u>ce qu</u>'on met dans le gombo. (object)
3. <u>Ce qui</u> m'intéresse surtout comme musique, c'est le jazz. (subject)
4. <u>Ce qu</u>'on va manger ce soir est super! (object)
5. Dis-moi vite <u>ce qui</u> est arrivé! (subject)
6. Ils m'ont servi <u>ce que</u> je voulais. (object)

C. 1. Tu ne nous a pas dit <u>ce que</u> tu as vu en Louisiane.
2. <u>Ce qui</u> me plaît ici, c'est les grands arbres et les maisons de style colonial.
3. Tu sais <u>ce qui</u> est arrivé à Julien? Il a perdu son portefeuille!
4. <u>Ce qu</u>'elle n'aime pas du tout, c'est les plats épicés.
5. Je ne sais pas <u>ce que</u> je vais prendre. Tout a l'air si bon!
6. <u>Ce qui</u> prend beaucoup de temps, c'est de préparer un gombo.

D. Answers will vary. Possible answer: In the first sentence, **ce qui** is used because it is the subject of the verb **passionne**. In the second sentence, **ce que** is used because it is the object of the verb **mettre**.

Answers

CHAPITRE 12

■ USING THE FUTURE

A. 1. When I finish high school, I will travel.
2. As soon as the guests leave, we will get some sleep.
3. When Martin arrives, we will celebrate.
4. The ship will depart as soon as everyone is on board.
5. Candace will return to work when she recovers from the accident.
6. Mrs. Sanders will retire as soon as the company finds a replacement.

B. 1. Quand tu iras aux Jeux olympiques, tu seras content.
2. Je serai heureuse dès que j'arriverai.
3. Quand on rentrera à la maison, je me coucherai.
4. Dès que tu trouveras le temps, tu viendras nous voir.
5. Sophie cherchera un emploi quand elle aura son diplôme.
6. Dès que les cours seront finis, nous partirons en vacances.
7. Quand il neigera, on construira un bonhomme de neige.

C. 1. Quand tu seras en France, tu verras beaucoup de petites voitures.
2. Je vous écrirai dès que j'arriverai là-bas.
3. Nous irons au café quand nous aurons le temps.
4. Dès que Josique apprendra la nouvelle, elle nous téléphonera.
5. Quand ils sauront que je suis ici, ils viendront me voir.
6. Qu'est-ce que vous ferez quand vous aurez 25 ans?

D. Answers will vary. Possible answers:
1. Quand je serai en vacances, je partirai en France.
2. Quand j'aurai dix-huit ans, je trouverai un appartement.
3. Dès que j'aurai mon diplôme, j'irai à l'université
4. Quand j'aurai assez d'argent, j'achèterai un ordinateur.
5. Quand j'aurai trente ans, je serai marié.
6. Dès que j'aurai une nouvelle voiture, je sortirai plus.
7. Quand j'aurai des enfants, je ferai du sport avec eux.
8. Quand j'aurai le temps, j'apprendrai à jouer de la guitare.

E. Answers will vary. Possible answers
It makes sense to have both clauses in the future since both events are to happen in the future.